DUMBING
DOWN
AMERICA

A Passionate Call to Fix America's School Systems

DUMBING DOWN AMERICA

THE WAR ON OUR NATION'S BRIGHTEST YOUNG MINDS
(AND WHAT WE CAN DO TO FIGHT BACK)

James R. Delisle

PRUFROCK PRESS INC
WACO, TEXAS

DEDICATION

This book is dedicated to three of my heroes:

◇ Dr. James J. Gallagher, who led a life of professional integrity and, in doing so, imbued in me the importance of this vital quality.

◇ Dr. Annemarie Roeper, my "gifted grandmother," who taught me well and often to pay as much attention to the hearts of gifted children as we do their minds.

◇ Matt Sewick, my "maple sugar kid," who showed me in my first years of teaching that giftedness may be hidden under all kinds of misbehaviors. Matt, you led me on a journey that continues today.

ACKNOWLEDGEMENT

Abundant thanks go to my editor, Lacy Compton, who is both precise and kind—two qualities that made my writing of this book a pleasant challenge.

Prufrock Press Inc.
P.O. Box 8813
Waco, TX 76714-8813
Phone: (800) 998-2208
Fax: (800) 240-0333
http://www.prufrock.com

TABLE OF CONTENTS

THREE REASONS TO CARE

On the first day of fourth grade, Jeff's teacher asked him what he would like to learn in school that he hadn't yet studied.

"Nuclear physics," answered Jeff, "because my third-grade teacher didn't understand it."

Apparently, neither did Jeff's fourth-grade teacher. Still, the two persevered as the year went along, with Jeff being allowed to introduce his teacher to the difference between a *quark* and a *lepton*. Subatomic particles became part of their shared vocabulary.

In fifth grade, Jeff's teacher was a kind man. Kind, but overwhelmed. He had never worked with someone as gifted as Jeff, and his solution was to require that Jeff do more work if he finished his assignments early. Not different work, just more of the same type of work. The topic of *quarks* never arose. Jeff achieved at minimal levels and parent-teacher conferences were filled with pleas for Jeff to "work up to his potential."

Middle school brought more boredom Jeff's way, as his meager grades in elementary school relegated him to low-level classes. Jeff didn't misbehave, he just found ways to cope: truancy, smoking pot, cutting himself. By the end of Jeff's ninth-grade year, his GPA was less than 1.0 and, the day he turned 16, Jeff left school forever. His study of nuclear physics was but a distant memory of a bygone time.

Morgan was the picture of success: class valedictorian, class president, and active involvement in multiple school clubs. How proud everyone was of her, even if she was not very proud of herself.

"In the pit of my stomach, I felt a deep sense of unaccomplishment," Morgan recalls. "Despite my many awards, I knew the truth: I had never written a paper any earlier than the night before it was due, and 'studying' for me consisted of cracking open my textbook for only the second or third time in that semester. The glowing sense of victory I had always expected to show up at high school graduation had stood me up."

Here's one reason why, based on Morgan's memories of one of her classes:

> One of my social studies teachers walked into the room, clapping his hands brusquely. "Okay, class, we have 3 weeks until the end of the school year and 10 chapters to cover. Turn to the section on the Korean War."
>
> We opened our books.
>
> "All right," he continued, "Now raise your right hand and place it palm down over the first page."
>
> We looked around at each other, confused, but followed his instructions.
>
> "Now, we've *covered* it," said the teacher, his chins jiggling as he chuckled through his pun. "Let's move on."
>
> "We're not going to learn about the Korean War?" protested one student.
>
> "You don't need to know about the Korean War unless you're Korean," the teacher responded.
>
> A hand shot up in the back of the class: "I'm Korean."
>
> "Oh . . . well, you can read that chapter on your own," responded the teacher. (Galbraith & Delisle, 2011, p. 123)

This was Morgan's AP American History class.

Justin was an 18-year-old college freshman on the verge of dropping out. A constant daydreamer growing up, he was diagnosed with ADHD and called an "underachiever" by many of his teachers. "But," he explains, "what can you achieve in an environment where you are not challenged and lose interest quickly?"

Justin recalls being 2 years old and using blocks to create elaborate train-like structures that were 10–30 feet in length. "I still have pictures!" Justin states. When school began, he found himself seldom paying attention to his kindergarten teacher, initially out of boredom, then out of anger: "She knew I could read, but that wasn't convenient because none of the other kids could. So I just sat there and 'learned' my alphabet letters."

Other than a fourth-grade teacher who allowed Justin to explore reading and math through technology, much of Justin's schooling mirrored his kindergarten experience: boredom and lack of relevance. Middle and high school brought fights, social isolation, and a withdrawal from reality. "I continued to daydream—all day every day. My two greatest releases were computer games and surfing Internet porn."

Taking an online IQ test at age 17, Justin discovered his aptitude was in the top 1%—his IQ score was 136. Now, in his freshman year at a community college, the intellectual joy and rigor everyone told Justin awaited him once he got to college was lacking. The educational Holy Grail remained elusive.

Justin recalls:

> Since a very young age, I couldn't wait to be an adult, so I could get the respect I thought I deserved. I'm full of questions about life, not just some material I'm supposed to memorize from a textbook. I craved some connection and didn't get it. I guess you could say I'm searching for a purpose—that is what drives me and, when I find it, it will guide me.

Justin's search continues.

Sadly, the three cases on the previous pages are not outliers, as gifted children across America are being fed pabulum of rehashed curriculum that does little to nourish their intellectual curiosity. Year after year, gifted children are the recipients of school content and practices aimed for an audience of average or below-average learners. No Child Left Behind forgot one vital group: gifted kids. As stated by educational pioneer James J. Gallagher in 1975:

> Failure to help the gifted child reach his potential is a societal tragedy, the extent of which is difficult to measure but which is surely great. How can we measure the sonata unwritten, the curative drug undiscovered, the absence of political insight? They are the difference between what we are and what we could be as a society. (p. 9)

More than a generation later, Gallagher's words are as true and insightful as ever.

AMERICA'S EDUCATIONAL CRISIS: IGNORING GIFTED CHILDREN

The word "crisis" is often overused in our society, as if having a bad hair day is equal in importance to Iran's acquisition of a nuclear bomb. Educators are no less apt to create crises than other professionals, so that some very substantive issues such as the achievement gap, the digital divide, and the presence of school violence seem to portend just as lousy a future for America as does the designation of ketchup as a vegetable in school lunches.

As defined on Dictionary.com, "crisis" has multiple meanings, including these:

1. a stage in a sequence of events at which the trend of all future events, especially for better or worse, is determined; a turning point

2. a dramatic emotional or circumstantial upheaval in a person's life

In the case of gifted children in America's schools today, both definitions apply, for although the educational metacrisis that finds gifted children performing at levels far below their capability is one concern, the individual microcrisis of a child like Jeff or Morgan or Justin is equally as important—and equally as tragic.

How did we get here? *When* did we arrive at the place, as a society, where providing instruction commensurate with a gifted child's abilities was construed as being unnecessary ("Gifted kids'll make it on their own—let's spend money on kids who are *truly* in need."), elitist ("Everyone is gifted in some way, you know . . ."), or racist ("You only want gifted programs to keep the middle-class White kids apart from minorities.")? The answers to these questions lie not only within the field of education, but are also explained by America's "pull yourself up by the bootstraps" ideology on which the founding of our nation was based. With countless examples of individuals who have made good lives for themselves despite poor economic conditions or less-than-ideal life circumstances, coupled with *other* countless examples of individuals whose life of privilege did not guarantee their eventual success, there has never been—and there still is not—a confluence of evidence or opinion that serving gifted children *actually matters*. So if we can't guarantee that extra efforts made on behalf of gifted children always work, then, critics contend, there must be *another* reason that advocates fight so valiantly to educate gifted children: to separate the educational chaff from the wheat, thereby incubating a privileged class of learners while leaving the rest to muddle in the mire. Is it no wonder, then, that John C. Gowan, a psychologist who specialized in serving gifted children in the mid-20th century, once remarked that the education of gifted children in America is "a passionless issue in a society geared to emergencies"?

Every gifted student needs to be valued first as a person and then as an
  individual who needs
Quality learning experiences that challenge and enrich their
Understanding of the world around them and facilitate the delicate
Intricacies of how their lives are woven into the
Tapestry of life that may confront them with joys as well as disappointments
Yet provides them with the resiliency to lead fulfilling lives.

Patricia S. Rendon, Coordinator for Gifted and Talented Programs,
Region One Education Service Center, Edinburg, TX

BUT I DIGRESS

In further chapters of this book, I will analyze three aspects
of the field of gifted child education: the upsides, the downsides,
and the next sides. Issues related to identifying gifted children and
providing for their educational and emotional needs in public schools
will be reviewed from an historical context, but the majority of
time will be spent on addressing the unfounded criticisms of gifted
child education from so-called "experts" who have a philosophical
ax to grind. (Ironically, many of those who oppose gifted education
programs also predominantly hail from such "elitist" institutions as
Harvard and Stanford. Hmmmm.) More than anything, I hope to
convey through this book the importance of saving smart kids from
educational structures that seem stacked against them, educational
reforms that are more concerned about measuring the stump than the
tree, and educational visionaries whose sight is hampered by the gauzy
lens of professional ignorance. Sprinkled throughout the book will
be comments from gifted education specialists, parents, students, and
others whose firsthand accounts of what gifted children need in order
to flourish will add texture and substance to the grim statistics cited.
Comments like these:

What bothers me most about school is the tremendous challenge I face with a curriculum that focuses only on passing state competency exams. "Teaching to the test" functionally shuts down advanced abilities.

—15-year-old boy, Alabama

There is a total disconnect between what people think I should know and what I am capable of learning. I want to soar, not wallow in a trough of indifference.

—17-year-old girl, Virginia

The title of this book, *Dumbing Down America*, is neither hyperbole nor exaggeration, for it appears that the educational establishments that are supposed to support and extol excellence are doing their best to make certain that America's gifted kids go nowhere fast. It is my hope that this book will serve as a clarion call to pay attention to the needs of our nation's most neglected minority: gifted children.

CHAPTER 1

IN THE BEGINNING

Natural ability without education has more often attained to glory and virtue than education without natural ability.
—Cicero

Anyone who believes that identifying gifted children and providing educational options for them is a new idea or a passing fad has either a short memory or a limited grasp of history. As Joanne Rand Whitmore (1980) pointed out more than 30 years ago,

> In the early recorded history of various cultures there is considerable evidence that youngsters possessing exceptionally advanced mental abilities were recognized when rather young, were highly prized, and were segregated from the masses for special educational treatment. (p. 4)

Whitmore (1980) went on to point out that the philosopher Plato advocated testing children for potential giftedness (although the term itself, *gifted*, was not used then) and, once found, preparing them for leadership roles by providing advanced educational opportunities. Going against the grain of the time, when leaders were selected exclusively from society's aristocracy, this egalitarian approach

1

recognized that high intelligence was due to something more than how wealthy or renowned your parents were. Clark (1997) added that similar quests for locating giftedness in children were sponsored by governments in ancient Egypt, Rome, China, and Japan.

This "talent search" continued in both the Holy Roman Empire and with the 15th-century Ottomans. Around 800 A.D., Charlemagne urged that the state look for high intelligence among all castes of society and, when found, that these children be educated at government expense. Ditto in Turkey, where a school for boys who were superior in strength, appearance, and intelligence was established at Topkapi Palace. And in 1648, the Czech educator and reformer, Jan Amos Komensky (Comenius) wrote *The Great Didactic*, a text that proposed 80 axioms that should guide a teacher's actions. Among the axioms?

◇ We do not learn what we already know

◇ Do not postpone the instruction of one who is ready to receive it

Both of these have relevance today in the education of gifted children.

The Renaissance brought attention to the need for patrons to support artists, sculptors, and musicians. Perhaps the greatest example of a patron recognizing the gifts of an individual and sponsoring his education is found in the life of Leonardo da Vinci (Gelb, 2004). Born to an unwed mother in 1452, da Vinci was not allowed membership in the Guild of Notaries, to which his father belonged, making him ineligible to follow in the professional footsteps of his father and grandfather. Instead, da Vinci became an apprentice with master sculptor and painter Andrea del Verrocchio. The small inclusion of an angel and a bit of landscape painted by da Vinci in one of his mentor's paintings caught the eye of Lorenzo de' Medici—and the rest, as they say, is history: Leonardo da Vinci came to be recognized as one of the greatest geniuses of all time. A wise and generous someone—de' Medici—stepped in to help an individual whose gifts were recognized as being superior.

Another example of an individual whose interest in intellectual prowess caused him to support a child of promise can be found in the life of physician Jean Itard. In the late 18th century, Itard found a young boy, about age 12, in the forests of central France. This boy had no known history, and no language. His behaviors were crude, yet Itard believed that this boy, whom he named Victor, survived in the woods due to his instincts and innate intelligence. For many years, Itard tried to educate and socialize Victor, with little success. Eventually, Itard abandoned this social experiment—and Victor himself—leaving him under the care of the nursemaid who had watched over him for years.

Given the lack of success of Itard's experiment, what part does this play in the growth of educating gifted children? Plenty. For, in addition to trying to educate this feral child, Itard also kept a diary—a day-by-day chronicle of Victor's intellectual growth and learning patterns. Eventually published as *The Wild Boy of Aveyron* (later a movie, François Truffaut's *The Wild Child*), this social experiment became one of the earliest attempts to capture those elements that cause a young child's mind to develop. As I wrote in an earlier publication, "to this day, Itard's work remains the sine qua non of studies that have the goal of exploring the development of individual talents" (Delisle, 1992, p. 2).

MEANWHILE, IN AMERICA

These schools to be under a visitor, who is annually to chuse a boy, of best genius in the school, of those whose parents are too poor to give them further education, and to send him forward to one of the grammar schools, of which twenty are proposed to be erected in different parts of the country, for teaching Greek, Latin, geography, and the higher branches of numerical arithmetic. Of the boys thus sent in any one year, trial is to be made at the grammar schools one or two years, and the best genius of the whole selected, and continued six years, and the residue dismissed. By this means twenty of the best geniuses will be raked from the rubbish annually, and

be instructed, at the public expence, so far as the grammar schools go.
—Thomas Jefferson, 1784

OK, so his choice of the words "rubbish" and "residue" may be an inarticulate way to describe nongifted children, but Jefferson's mission is clear: to identify and educate intelligent children in ways that respect their fine minds. And by limiting his search to families too poor to educate their children, Jefferson opens up the doors to excellence by recognizing what his ancient Greek and Chinese counterparts knew centuries earlier: Giftedness can be found in all strata of society.

So how *exactly* is one to identify potential genius? Must we rely solely on the observations of others, who may or may not know a gifted child when they see one? The answer (one answer, at least) lies in what began to happen in the latter half of the 19th century, when interest in intelligence coincided with the advent of a branch of ancient philosophy that became its own science in the 1870s: psychology.

Although educators and psychologists seemed to agree, in principle, on what intelligence looked like, no one was entirely certain that something so amorphous could actually be measured. So, the government of France asked psychologist Alfred Binet to devise a way to distinguish between children who were educable and those who were not capable of academic advancement. Instead of designing assessments tied in with specific content such as math or reading skills, Binet (and his colleague, Theodore Simon) devised tests that measured qualities such as attention, memory, and judgment—the underlying foundations of learning, if you will. After many test administrations in which children scored at widely varying levels of competence, Binet and Simon established cut-off scores for the following categories of learners: idiots, imbeciles, and normals. These terms were mere descriptors, not carrying the pejorative impact that they do in today's parlance, and thus began an era where children were ranked by a particular test score number—on the Binet-Simon Scale.

Enter Lewis M. Terman. As an undergraduate psychology major at Indiana University in the early 20th century, Terman became interested in the range of intelligence—from "idiot" on up. For his senior seminar project, he wrote two reports: one on mental deficiency and one on superior intelligence. Through this work, Terman became acquainted with the recently published Binet-Simon Scale. Once enrolled in a doctoral program at Clark University, Terman continued to explore the world of intelligence, comparing two groups of boys: those who were "mentally backward" and those who had high intelligence, as measured by the Binet-Simon Scale. In one of his retrospectives, Terman (1954) stated that "the experiment contributed little or nothing to science, but it contributed a lot to my future thinking" (p. 222). *That* would be an understatement!

Shortly thereafter, while on the faculty at Stanford University, Terman revised the Binet-Simon Scale and, in 1916, published the first Stanford-Binet Intelligence Test, an individual test that resulted in an "intelligence quotient"—IQ—that became a measurement prototype so strong that it is still in use today, a century later.

In publishing this test, Terman achieved the "professional cred" he needed to pursue his long-held ambition: to explore the world of exceptional intelligence. So, armed with a grant from the Commonwealth Fund of New York City, he was challenged to locate and study children whose IQ's were in the "genius" range—140 and above. Terman found 1,528 such children—and he continued to follow their educational and life progress for decades, resulting in psychology's most eminent longitudinal study, the five-volume *Genetic Studies of Genius.*

Much has been written about Terman's legacy, and it is not all positive (Leslie, 2000), as his subjects were predominantly White and middle class, yet he applied his generalizations about intelligence to everyone. As time passed, the identities of some of his "Termites" (as they came to be called) were revealed, including Jess Oppenheimer, creator and writer for *I Love Lucy*, Edward Drmytryk, a film director whose credits include *The Caine Mutiny*, and Lee Cronbach, noted psychologist and former President of the American Psychological Association. Hundreds of patents, books, and inventions are credited to this august group of 1,528 and, as Terman (1954) reflected later in his career, "no one developed post-adolescent stupidity" (p. 227). This tongue-in-cheek comment actually is one of Terman's more important findings, as the 19th-century belief in "early ripe, early rot" (i.e., if you use too much of your finite mind too soon, you'll have nothing left for the later years) was discarded into the bin of false truths. Intelligence, it seems, was a lifelong attribute—gifted once, gifted always.

AND THEN THERE WAS LETA

Thousands of miles away from Stanford, in New York City, another psychologist with an interest similar to Terman's emerged: Leta S. Hollingworth. Beginning her study of gifted children in the same year that the Stanford-Binet was published (1916), Hollingworth did what Terman did not: She examined the intellectual, emotional, and educational lives of the most highly gifted children of all—those whose IQs were above 180.

Her background was as a schoolteacher and principal and, although she eventually received a Ph.D. in psychology, her ties to the classroom were always obvious in her work. In 1922, she convinced the New York City School Board to fund a program for the district's most highly capable children. Years later, in 1937, she became a teacher at Speyer School, P.S. 500, where she worked extensively with children whose IQs ranged from 130–200. In a book that documents her work with these unique young children, Hollingworth (1942) stated that "the minds of these children are occupied primarily with exploration of the world in which they have recently arrived . . . This is the golden age of the intellect" (p. 292).

"You'll just have to wait 'til we get there." "Show your work." "Show me the steps each time." "No, you may not work ahead; stay with the class." What is wrong with each of these statements is what troubles public education for gifted learners in America. We should be placing an ever-increasing importance on moving our brightest students ahead by using a pace appropriate to their individual needs—not asking them to wait until others catch up. Sadly, we stifle creativity and eagerness with these "worst practices." Readiness needs to be applied to all. Rethink it, America!

Ruthi Manning-Freeman, public educator since 1975, Breckenridge, CO

What sets Hollingworth's work apart from Terman's can be encapsulated thusly: She believed that to be *precocious* was to be *vulnerable*. When children have the intelligence of an adult but the emotions of a child, certain special problems might arise. They include:

◇ *problems of play and friendship*, as the gifted child's vocabulary, preference for complicated games, and the importance of rules may not be appreciated by less able children of the same age;

◇ *problems associated with a lackluster school curriculum*, as Hollingworth (1942) believed that children with IQs of 140 waste half their time in school, while those with IQs above 170 spend their time doing "various sorts of bizarre and wasteful activities" (p. 299) under the guise of "learning";

◇ *problems in becoming negative toward authority figures*, especially when gifted children feel compelled to "make good" the mistakes or misperceptions of adults and are told to "mind their manners" instead of being taken seriously for their accurate, astute insights;

◇ *problems of using their intellect to take advantage of others*, which Hollingworth labeled as "benign chicanery," or when gifted children laud their intellect over less-competent others to get their way. Hollingworth conceded that this is a skill mastered by many savvy adults, yet she is cautious when children use it to their advantage, as it may set them apart as loners, which gets back to her initial concern about play and friendships.

In her lifetime, Hollingworth's work never received the recognition it deserved and, being a female, she was seldom taken seriously by foundation directors who could have funded her projects. Still, in retrospect, Hollingworth's work is as groundbreaking as was Terman's. She was just born in an era when her achievements were hijacked by her gender.

THE EBB AND FLOW OF EDUCATING GIFTED CHILDREN

With two such powerful proponents of gifted children as Terman and Hollingworth, you'd think that the momentum to continue their research legacies would move forward in a straight-line, upward trajectory.

Well, guess again.

More than any other area of special education, gifted child education has been seen as expendable, not essential. So, when times get tough and money gets scarce, gifted programs are often on the chopping block for reasons alluded to earlier—elitism, racism, or being deemed as an unnecessary luxury. And whereas children with disabilities are a sympathetic group for whom to advocate, it's harder to advocate for a category of learner—gifted kids—who appear to be successful in school already.

In addition to an overall apathy that many people—including many educators—have about providing services for gifted students, proponents of gifted child education find themselves in a political maelstrom as well. So, when our nation is in a collective crisis mode, gifted child education thrives, while it declines when politicos aren't as concerned about our country's future.

There is no better example of gifted child education being used as a political football than the Russian launch of the Sputnik satellite in 1957. When this happened, America's dominance of everything scientific came into question. Was it *even possible* that those dreaded and feared Russians might, in fact, get to the moon before we did? Perish the thought! Seemingly overnight, a clarion call was made to upgrade the education system, especially in math and science, so that the United States would be second to none. Countless grants were written and millions of dollars spent to design curriculum that would challenge our nation's most astute students and, in 1958, the National Defense Education Act (P.L. 85-864) was enacted by Congress—the surest sign yet that gifted children and their education were top priorities.

For a few years, anyway. But when the Civil Rights Movement began in earnest in the 1960s, gifted child education became a back-burner issue. In the tug of war between equity and excellence, equity won. It became downright difficult to be an advocate for gifted kids, as those who did support gifted programs were perceived as taking money away from kids who *really* needed it. Also, it didn't help that the majority of children being identified as gifted resembled Terman's sample—White and middle class—more so than the racial mixture of our nation, leaving the perception that even though "separate but equal" was ruled unconstitutional, it was alive and well in gifted child education programs. Gifted child educators came to be seen as the new segregationists.

The pendulum shifted back a bit in 1972, when a Congressionally financed report called *Education of the Gifted and Talented* was published by the U.S. Commissioner of Education, Sidney Marland. Among the Marland Report's findings were these:

◇ there were approximately 2 million gifted children in America, with only a small fraction being served in special programs;

◇ more than 50% of gifted children were not performing at levels equal to their intelligence;

◇ more than 50% of school administrators believed they had *no* gifted children in their schools;

◇ only 21 states had any legislation specific to gifted children, and even those laws were weak and ineffective—the federal government played *no* role whatsoever; and

◇ teacher preparation programs in the area of gifted child education were few in number.

Indeed, the Marland Report's gloomy findings did have one bright spot: the conclusion was reached that when special educational opportunities are afforded to gifted children, and the pace of instruction is increased, the social and emotional difficulties that gifted children face in school disappear.

As a result of this increased exposure to the needs of gifted children, the federal government established an Office of Gifted and Talented (OGT) for the first time in 1975. With a separate director and a dedicated budget (granted, only $2.5 million to start), gifted children had, for once, an advocate in Washington, DC. Throughout the country, at both state and local levels, gifted child education programs began to surge—but not for long.

Another Congressional Act, the Education and Consolidation Improvement Act of 1981, took 30 distinct federal offices, including OGT, and dismantled them. In their stead, a competitive block grant program was established, in which the 30 agencies now had to compete for the limited funds available and, as many predicted would happen, interest in and funding for gifted programs diminished. Once again, other kids with *real* needs took precedence over the perceived *lack* of need for gifted program services.

Another positive blip in the history of gifted child education occurred with the 1988 passage of the Jacob K. Javits Gifted and Talented Education Act (P.L. 100-297), which provided $7.9 million in large, multiyear grants to universities and school districts who sought to identify and educate "historically underrepresented populations" of gifted children, including children of color, children in poverty, and "twice-exceptional" children who had both giftedness and a particular disability. At the same time, The National Research Center on the Gifted and Talented was established, housed at the University of Connecticut, with satellite offices located at various other universities.

The Javits program continued until 2011, when its funding was eliminated due to a Congressional study that found it (and many other educational programs) had little impact on the intended student populations. However, despite this elimination, the Javits program was funded again in 2014 with a $5 million federal appropriation. A drop in the bucket, perhaps, but in this era of fiscal austerity, it's surprising that any new money would be given, especially to a program that was seen as being inconsequential by evaluators just a few years prior.

Other events and publications have certainly influenced this ebb and flow of services to gifted children (see Chapter 2), but one thing is certain: Although no educated, thoughtful individual would ever question whether math should be taught in schools, and although no elementary school principal ever has to answer the question, "Do we *really* need to have fifth grade?", the issue of whether gifted child education is important—indeed, whether it should exist *at all*—is likely to remain a sticking point in this always controversial field of study. Apparently, no one perceived that "excellence" and "equity" are not opposites but rather, they are two sides of the same coin; for when a child—any child—is provided the tools needed to succeed to the max, this is an example of excellence in action. The equity piece of this equation comes about when we recognize that it takes different steps and strategies for kids of varying abilities to reach their goals. What could be more equitable than promoting excellence through various methods?

SO WHY THIS HISTORY LESSON?

Who knew that a field of study as contemporary as gifted child education had its roots in ancient cultures? This age-old fascination with children who pushed the boundaries of what it meant to be smart has gone through more permutations than a chameleon in a paint factory. And still, centuries after it was first examined, the central questions remain: What, *exactly*, is giftedness, can it be defined precisely, and if we can define and identify it, is it really essential to nurture it through special school programs?

Don't hold back! If a 10-year-old is ready for a calculus class, arrange it for her. Other than a minimum legal age for some activities, services, or privileges, age never matters as much as it does in school. Age and ability are not a required match in real-world applications of giftedness. While there is much to support talent development and the value of practice, there is no minimum age one must reach to demonstrate exceptional knowledge or abilities in any subject area or activity. Let students progress through K–12 curriculum at a pace consistent with abilities, not age.

Colleen Harsin, Director, Davidson Academy of Nevada, Reno, NV

At first, there were no numbers to consider, no IQ scores to pore over, as individual cultures determined intelligence based upon their own societal needs and proclivities. Surely, in an agrarian culture, the "most intelligent" members would be considered those who brought fallow fields to fruition and found new ways to get water to barren acres. In a society where intellect was measured by how well one could carry on a logical, passionate conversation, the philosophers and deep thinkers would occupy the status as the most intelligent. And in a place and time where artistic expression was considered the highest form of accomplishment, the painters and musicians of the day would qualify as being innately capable and creative.

But still, even after IQ tests became prominent and people's intellects could be ranked by a two- or three-digit number, the controversy over what constitutes giftedness continued. Part of this is due to the fact that we still live in a culturally complex and diverse world, so that being a gifted child in suburban Connecticut differs markedly from being a gifted kid growing up in the Amazonian rainforest. As observed by anthropologist Stanley Garn, "If an aborigine drafted an IQ test, all of Western civilization would presumably flunk it."

So if not IQ . . . then what? And given that there appear to be so many ways that humans can express their intelligence—through words, numbers, actions—should the field of gifted child education be limited to a few, or opened up to the many? If we identify 3%–5% of any population as being gifted (which is commonly done in schools today), is that being too stingy? If we say that up to 25% of a population can be gifted at any one time (as some theorists espouse), given the right circumstances, is this diluting the gifted label to the point of meaninglessness? What about kids who test out at the highest levels of intelligence, yet do poorly in school—should they be considered gifted at all, or must these individuals "prove" their giftedness regularly by performing consistently as top achievers?

Here's the good news: Answers to these questions are easy to find. Here's the bad news: Very few people seem to agree which answers are correct.

Perhaps this confusion over the definition of the term itself—gifted—is what has caused this endeavor to have so many fits and starts over time. It is hard to serve gifted children well when we can't even agree on who they are, and it is difficult to advocate for a special population of learners when we can't effectively argue that our efforts on their behalf will guarantee positive results.

Upsides and downsides . . . the field of gifted child education has plenty of both.

CHAPTER 2

THE UPSIDES

> *We are altogether too easily deceived by the time-worn argument that the gifted student, "the genius," perhaps, will get along somehow without much teaching. The fact is, the gifted... the brilliant... are the ones who need the closest attention of the skillful mechanic.*
>
> —W. Franklin Jones, 1912

When Santiago Gonzales—"Santi"—was an infant, his parents moved from Mexico to Colorado. It is the nature of parenthood to believe you have a "smart kid," but Santiago's parents had proof positive: At 18 months old, Santi recited the alphabet and, by age 2, he could count to 20 in three languages. Seeking a school that would let Santi explore his interests at his own pace, his parents enrolled him in a Montessori preschool that fit the bill perfectly, as Santi's teacher indulged his interests in fractions, rocks, and minerals. By kindergarten, Santi was exploring the Big Bang Theory of cosmic creation—all was good.

Until first grade. Then, Santi's teacher required that he complete basic math and reading assignments. The work was simple, and Santi grew frustrated. After testing showed Santi to have a very high IQ, a local private school admitted him to a third- to fourth-grade class at the age of 7. Things went well for 3 years when, as unhappy luck would have it, Santi's next teacher disallowed his intellectual strivings and required Santi to complete work he had mastered years earlier. In Santi's words, this teacher was like a "vacuum that didn't suck well— pretty useless" (Schultz & Delisle, 2012, p. 123). Frustrated with where to go next, Santi's mom brought him to Arapahoe Community College, where he was admitted at the age of 10, based on his entrance exam scores. Today, Santi is a full-time student at the Colorado School of Mines, majoring in computer science and math, a dual degree he will finish at age 16.

THE NONSUCKING VACUUM

In the field of gifted child education, it seems that every uplifting story like Santi's has an underbelly of angst. Rather than receiving instruction at a level commensurate with his abilities, Santi (and his parents) had to fight time after time, teacher after teacher, to ensure that his abilities were respected. Just as an avalanche proceeds down a slope at its own, organic pace, unhampered by the obstacles it confronts, intellect demands the same freedom. Time after time, though, the obstacles prevail when the needs of gifted children go unaddressed.

This chapter is devoted to the "upsides" of gifted child education; the people, programs, and grand ideas that offer hope to gifted children that they will learn something new *because* of school not *in spite* of it. Yet it would be both naïve and incorrect to gloss over the glaring inconsistencies that exist even within the best-laid plans. In too many cases, a stunning program for gifted students collapses after a change in administration brings a new direction; a promising practice that allows

A gifted child needs TIME. Time to be a gifted kid, and time to be a kid. These "times" may overlap; they may also be distinct. A gifted child needs opportunities to learn, explore, delve, and stretch in a quest for knowledge. A gifted kid needs time to dream, wonder, and ponder the eccentricities of life and the existential aspects of our world. A gifted kid needs time to play, grow, hurt, and enjoy. Gifted kids need the emotional support of caring adults and peers who love them for who they are and help them find these "times" to develop an entity as a gifted individual.

Ed Amend, Licensed Psychologist, Lexington, KY

gifted children to be placed in classes based on their abilities, not their ages, is eliminated when an ill-informed, credentialed someone states that such acceleration causes social and emotional harm to children; or a university-based program for gifted high school students is curtailed when a fear of liability for underage students on campus causes high anxiety with the university lawyers. It's hard to build and sustain momentum when gifted child education programs are treated like whimsical fads rather than the essential services that they are. Every time an educator, attorney, or politician allows illogic or bias to guide the decision to educate gifted children appropriately or not, America becomes what we can ill afford: a little dumber.

Still, optimism has good reason to prevail, as individuals outside of the mainstream of gifted child education are calling for action for our nation's most capable youth. For example, Chester Finn and Jessica Hockett, in their 2012 book *Exam Schools*, looked at 165 U.S. public high schools that cater to the needs of gifted learners. Yet as Finn wrote in an op-ed piece, "Young, Gifted and Neglected," which appeared in *The New York Times* in 2012: "America should have 1,000 or more high schools for able students, not 165, and elementary and middle schools that spot and prepare their future pupils" (para. 16). Additionally, the Partnership for 21st Century Skills, a national organization with sponsors as diverse as Apple, Ford Motors, Cisco Systems, Crayola, and the National Education Association, have well-developed plans to synchronize the age-old "three R's" of curriculum content with the new "4 C's" needed for 21st-century learners:

◇ critical thinking and problem solving,
◇ communication,
◇ collaboration, and
◇ creativity and innovation.

These skills, coupled with enriched content devoted to global awareness and civic, economic, and environmental literacy, mesh the goals of general educators with those of gifted learners and their teachers. Other organizations have also called for emphasis on gifted learners. For example, the National Association for Gifted Children (NAGC) and the Association for Middle Level Education (formerly called The National Middle School Association), two groups that did not always see eye-to-eye when it comes to identifying and serving gifted children, produced a joint Position Statement in 2005 that supported, among other things, that all middle school teachers have "meaningful knowledge and understanding about the needs of gifted learners" (p. 2) and that all middle school teachers "provide curriculum, instruction and other opportunities to meet the needs of students with high ability" (p. 3).

This attention to the needs of gifted children by organizations that have vested interests in many students, not just gifted ones, is a positive step forward. Still, until such time that educators, politicians, and policy wonks are ready to spend what it takes in both human and financial capital to ensure that gifted children are not sidestepped in the reform process, the crisis for gifted education in America is all too real. A well-written position statement is one thing . . . but ensuring that it is acted upon in America's thousands of middle schools is quite another matter. In too many cases, U.S. middle schools are a "dead zone" for gifted programming, as gifted elementary programs (if they existed at all) have ended while high school honors and AP courses have yet to begin.

Let's examine some programs, research, and ideas that might guide their travels.

FROM *A NATION AT RISK* TO *A NATION DECEIVED*

Whatever your political persuasion, few would say that the administration of President Ronald Reagan was a high point in funding for the gifted education community. Under Reagan's watch, the Office of Gifted and Talented (OGT) was eliminated and its director reassigned. The small federal budget for OGT that had slowly grown to $7.5 since its inception in 1975 was reduced to $0 in 1981. Bleak days, indeed, for advocates of gifted children.

18

Ironically, a report that gained international attention was commissioned that same year, 1981, by then U.S. Secretary of Education, Terrel Bell. Led by Chairman David Pierpoint Gardner, the National Commission on Excellence in Education was charged with defining problems afflicting American education and recommending possible solutions to these problems.

The composition of the Commission's members was impressive, as it included university presidents, teachers and school administrators, CEOs of multinational corporations, school board members, former state governors, and even a Nobel Laureate, Dr. Glenn Seaberg.

Over many months, the Commissioners met eight times and also held six public forums on different areas of concern, including one meeting held at Harvard University that focused on gifted and talented students. More than 75 people (including your author, who at the time was a doctoral student) presented testimony, and the roster of speakers was a "Who's Who in Gifted" at the time: Joseph Renzulli, John Feldhusen, Dorothy Sisk, Julian Stanley, and James Gallagher, to name a few.

The Commission issued its report, *A Nation at Risk*, in April 1983 and, from the introductory comments on forward, American education was raked across the coals as being overly simplistic and substandard. No statement sums up the seriousness of the problem better than this one from the report's introduction:

> What was unimaginable a generation ago has begun to occur—other (nations) are matching and surpassing our educational attainments . . . If an unfriendly foreign power had attempted to impose on America the mediocre educational performance that exists today, we might well have viewed it as an act of war. (p. 9)

What brought such a strong reaction from the Commission members were statistics like these:

◇ more than half of all gifted students do not match their tested ability in school performance;

19

◇ more than 40% of high school students could not draw infer-
ences from written material;

◇ the majority of secondary school students had mastered 80%
of the content of their textbooks *before* ever opening them for
the school year;

◇ in not one of 19 academic measures that ranked the U.S. in
comparison with other nations did the U.S. score in first or
second place;

◇ school curricula, for the most part, focused on memorization
and acquisition of low-level skills, not on problem solving and
analysis; and

◇ teacher training is especially lacking in math, science, and foreign languages, as well as in programs that focus on methods
of teaching gifted students.

Stating that American education was "a rising tide of mediocrity"
(National Commission on Excellence in Education, 1983, p. 9), the
Commission wasn't afraid to mention the elephant in the room: that
curriculum in most schools and subjects was a mile wide and an inch
deep. "Coverage" was more important than "depth," with the end result
being a lackluster curriculum that let few students shine.

These and other conclusions by the Commission were eerily
reminiscent of the Marland Report's findings from a decade earlier
(and they are uncannily prescient of today's criticisms of American
education). However, upon the release of *A Nation at Risk*, there was a
seismic reaction to its publication—and its ominous findings. The title
alone gave this report an aura of gravitas. Far from being a government
publication that few read or cared about, this one made the rounds in
both print and electronic media—even Walter Cronkite addressed it
on his evening newscast! President Ronald Reagan touted this report
in speech after speech, raising education—at least in theory—as
America's top economic priority (Cavanaugh, 2004). (How ironic for a
leader who thought so little of the U.S. Department of Education that
he fought—unsuccessfully—to dismantle it during his administration.)

So with such widespread attention being given to the plight
of many aspects of America's educational system, including how it

undervalues gifted students, you'd assume that tons of new programs and money would be available to educate our most able children. Sorry, it didn't work out that way.

The main problem seemed to be that politicians and the general public focused so much on the report's negatives that they didn't spend time thinking through possible solutions. In commenting on *A Nation at Risk* two decades later, educator John Goodlad (2003) believed the report had plenty of smoke but no flames, and stated that its lack of attention to K–8 education (*A Nation at Risk* focused almost entirely on high school) doomed it from the start. Likewise, David Berliner and Bruce Biddle (1995) took exception to the report's conclusions, calling America's crisis in education a "manufactured crisis" that was nothing more than a politically charged assault on America's public schools. And in the U.S. Department of Education's 25-year retrospective on the impact of *A Nation at Risk*, then-Secretary of Education Margaret Spellings stated in *A Nation Accountable* that "we remain a nation at risk, but now we are a nation informed, a nation accountable, and a nation that recognizes there is much work to be done . . . for the first time in our history, we have reliable data to evaluate student performance" (U.S. Department of Education, 2008, p. 1). From my perspective, Spelling's comments and her lack of follow-through with specific, positive interventions amounted to all filler, no meat.

The remainder of *A Nation Accountable* focuses primarily on how the newly enacted No Child Left Behind (NCLB) law would return America to the educational prominence it had attained in previous generations. Graph after graph, statistic after statistic in this 25-year retrospective attended to topics such as the rising dropout rate and the low levels of reading and math proficiency in the preceding two and a half decades. Just one thing was missing: There was virtually no attention paid to gifted students. In fact, the word "gifted" is not used once in *A Nation Accountable*. Once again, our nation's most highly capable students were left on the sidelines; they never received the full promise of *A Nation at Risk*'s recommendations. The seismic shift in attitudes about gifted students that seemed so prominent in 1983 had melted away like snowflakes in May.

One step forward . . . two steps back. Our dumbness continues.

21

A NATION DECEIVED

But then, after yet-another period of widespread neglect for the needs of gifted students, a new report emerged—and this one had both teeth and money. Titled *A Nation Deceived: How Schools Hold Back America's Brightest Students* (Colangelo, Assouline, & Gross, 2004), this report was funded by the John Templeton Foundation to the tune of $361,000—a relatively small investment that yielded a huge return. Designed to examine the role of acceleration practices in America's schools, the final two-volume report (see http://www.nationdeceived.org to download the report) distilled hundreds of research-backed studies that enumerated the many forms of academic acceleration possible. Practices as diverse as grade skipping, early entrance to kindergarten or college, independent study of complex topics, and more than one dozen other forms of acceleration were reviewed. The result? In virtually every instance, acceleration was a workable, yet underused, way to serve academically gifted students. In fact, the report's authors were nonplussed when they discovered that they could find no other educational practice that is so well researched yet so rarely put to use.

Colangelo and colleagues (2004) listed 20 reasons that acceleration is often an optimal way to serve academically gifted students, including these:

- ◇ #1: Acceleration is the most effective curriculum intervention for gifted students.
- ◇ #3: Acceleration is a virtually cost-free intervention.
- ◇ #4: Gifted children tend to be socially and emotionally more mature than their agemates. For many bright students, acceleration provides a better personal maturity match with classmates.
- ◇ #6: Testing, especially above-level testing (using tests developed for older students) is highly effective in identifying students who would benefit from acceleration.
- ◇ #10: Gifted students entering college early experience both short-term and long-term academic success, leading to long-term occupational success and personal satisfaction.

So, backed by reams of solid research about the positive impact of acceleration, you'd think that teachers, administrators, and parents of gifted children would be strong advocates for such practices. Well, yes and no—for despite research evidence to the contrary, many individuals within education still hold biases against acceleration. As often happens in our world, when research results conflict with our personal opinions or experiences, we tend to dismiss the most valid barometer of all (the research results) and fall back onto our own beliefs. Case in point: In a four-page article in *TIME* Magazine (Thornburg, 2004) coinciding with the release of *A Nation Deceived*, a 34-year-old teacher who had been grade skipped during her elementary years said the following: "In high school, I was teased about being a virgin. Soon, I wanted to do the things my friends were doing, even though I was younger" (p. 58).

Although I empathize with this author's virginal angst, I find it hard to believe that a decision to place her with a group of slightly older kids at the age of 4 had as much bearing on the subsequent adolescent teasing as she recounts. And even if it did, what would have been the fallback position? Keeping this child (and thousands of others like her) in a class of agemates in kindergarten where she and her teacher were the only ones in the room capable of reading? The intellectual frustrations that she would have tolerated then, and in subsequent years, might have had an effect on her psyche that far overrode the importance of some stray comments from ignorant teens about her sexual inexperience.

Of course, there are some gifted kids for whom the most extreme form of acceleration—skipping one or more grade levels—is not an appropriate option; the authors of *A Nation Deceived* took great care in citing what these instances might look like. Several of this report's authors, and others, also revised the Iowa Acceleration Scale (IAS; Assouline, Colangelo, Lupkowski-Shoplik, Lipscomb, & Forstadt, 2009), an instrument that is used to calculate the possible benefits of whole-grade acceleration for students in grades K–8. Using the IAS, people no longer had to make judgments about acceleration based on "gut feelings" or personal biases; they could actually use a validated research tool to guide their decisions.

What *A Nation Deceived* did was to highlight the countless times when acceleration *is* an appropriate, cost-effective way to serve academically capable students in legitimate, respectful ways. One size may not fit all, in shoes or in education, but just as a pair of size 7 sneakers on a size 9 foot would cause bunions and other discomforts, an educational placement that is two sizes too small results in a student winching in pain from the torture of an improper fit between age and intellect.

The end result of *A Nation Deceived* was that acceleration practices moved from the back to the front burner in conversations about how to serve gifted children. It didn't hurt that the report's authors—all highly respected individuals with more than 100 years of collective experiences with gifted individuals—were perceived by their academic peers as scholars who did not have a particular educational ax to grind (. . . as some professionals in the gifted education field do); they simply wanted to do best for whatever gifted child happened to be sitting in front of them.

An added bonus: *A Nation Deceived* was commissioned at a time when the most exciting development in 30+ years of gifted education advocacy was just starting to blossom: the founding of the Davidson Institute for Talent Development.

THE POWER OF PRODIGIOUS THINKING

Jan Davidson was an entrepreneur right from the start: She began a tutoring service at the age of 13. In later years, Jan wondered why the emerging marvels of computer technology were not being used to teach kids on an individualized basis. After all, it was the late 1970s—surely every child didn't need to be on the same page of the same textbook throughout America's classrooms! So, in 1982, she founded a company, Davidson and Associates, that would bring educational software to the masses. And it did. If you've ever used Math Blasters or Reading Blasters, then you've been touched by the genius of Jan.

Jan's husband, Bob, had an MBA from UCLA, a juris doctorate from George Washington University, and was the executive vice president for engineering and construction with the global Parsons Corporation. Jan convinced him, in 1989, to leave Parsons and become

CEO of Davidson and Associates, where this dynamic duo continued to produce innovative and popular software, while partnering with companies such as Fisher Price and Simon & Schuster. By the time they sold their company in 1997, they had become wildly successful—and amazingly generous.

Turning their interests toward philanthropy, Jan and Bob did a 2-year analysis of what segments of the American population were being neglected most severely—and what they found must have surprised them, for in a nation so rich with talented scientists, writers, musicians, and mathematicians, the Davidsons discovered that highly gifted children were about the most neglected kids in America. Surely, if one had prodigious talents or intellectual or creative aptitudes, schools would be clamoring to do all they could do to make sure this nascent genius bloomed to full flower. When Jan and Bob found out that this was not the case, they took on the task themselves—and the world of gifted child education was changed forever.

The Davidson Institute for Talent Development (DITD) was founded in 1999 as a not-for-profit foundation whose stated goal is to support profoundly gifted children through information resources, networking and educational opportunities, family support, advocacy, and scholarships. Starting with the Young Scholars (YS) program and 15 highly gifted young children, YS has grown to now serve more than 2,000 gifted children and their families nationwide. But the YS program was just the beginning, as the Davidson's grasp of all-things-gifted has continued to grow in subsequent years. Here are just a few of the DITD programs offered:

⋄ The THINK Summer Institute is a 3-week residential program at the University of Nevada-Reno for 13- to 16-year-olds, who may earn up to 6 hours of college credit for the courses they take during this accelerated summer school.

⋄ The Davidson Academy of Nevada, an outgrowth of the THINK Institute, is a free, public charter school for gifted middle and high school students. A residential component was added recently to the day programs that are offered to more than 175 enrolled students.

◇ The Davidson Fellows is a scholarship program offering financial awards ranging from $10,000–$50,000 to students who complete an original, significant piece of work with the potential to make a positive societal contribution in any of the following areas: science, math, technology, music, literature, and "out of the box thinking," which combines any of the above disciplines. Having awarded more than $4 million to 184 Fellows in just over a decade, the Davidson Fellows Scholarship was rated with The United Negro College Fund, the Bill and Melinda Gates Foundation, and the Miss America Pageant as one of the "World's 10 Biggest Scholarships" by thebestcolleges.org in 2012.

◇ The Educators Guild is a free service to teachers, administrators, and counselors that connects them electronically with other professionals who have specific concerns about giftedness and gifted children.

◇ The Davidson Gifted Database includes hundreds of free, downloadable articles on virtually any aspect of giftedness, from perfectionism to identification to twice-exceptional children, who have both giftedness and a disability. The database (which is updated regularly) also has information on every state's policies and laws regarding gifted education.

As IQ increases, so does uniqueness. Thus, individualization is the key, and meeting the needs of the whole child is the goal. To this end, we need more emphasis on the profoundly gifted, creative thinkers—those who are driven to continually create, who have no tolerance for repetition, and who may or may not actually "produce" writing, painting, music, etc. While nurturing their creative minds, gifted programs must also focus on the importance of organizational skills, a strong work ethic, goal setting, and learning how to learn so that these kids will have the tools necessary to function successfully in society.

Cindy Crowe, university instructor and parent of a 20-something gifted child, Newburgh, IN

The Davidsons tackled a subset of the gifted population that few had focused on before: profoundly gifted children. (Yes, just as the range of mental retardation lies from mild to extreme, the same is true with giftedness.) What the Davidsons found was that the children most stifled by school, and those most isolated from true peers, were those whose minds raced 3 or more years ahead of their expected grade placement. Examples of such children are two of the Davidson Fellows from 2012:

◇ Sara Volz, age 17, was a $50,000 scholarship winner for her project titled "Enhancing Algae Biofuels," for which she developed a process that would increase the amount of oil produced naturally by algae to make algae-based biofuels more feasible—a truly "green" solution to our energy dilemma.

◇ Nathan Chen, age 18, was a $25,000 scholarship winner who completed a project called "The Importance of Passion," for which he created a cello portfolio that commented on what it means to be successful, with one key being the pursuit of one's passions.

Although the DITD is interested primarily in the highest-of-high gifted children, the effects of its work continue to have profound impacts on the entire gifted education field. Its website (http://www.davidsongifted.org) is arguably the most comprehensive of the thousands of other websites that target the gifted population; the publication of the Davidsons' book, *Genius Denied: How to Stop Wasting Our Brightest Young Minds*, in 2004 brought the issue of gifted children to an audience of lay readers who had not previously considered gifted children to be at risk in our schools; and their constant outreach efforts to schools, educators, and parents brought about by myriad suggestions and advice available through their vast array of services has provided both information and comfort to those who, heretofore, had few reliable places to turn.

If the field of gifted education had superheroes, Jan and Bob Davidson would both have magnificent capes. They'd also have another superhero for a friend: Jack Kent Cooke.

THE JACK KENT COOKE FOUNDATION

You might say that Jack Kent Cooke lived a life filled with color. A native of Ontario, he dropped out of high school to help his family financially during the Great Depression. Selling encyclopedias door to door for 3 years (starting at age 14), he came to know his way around the financial world, eventually managing newspapers and radio stations throughout Canada. Jack Kent Cooke was both an athlete and musician and, although not highly educated via the traditional university pathway, always respected intelligence—his own and others'. His mantra later became "Destiny demands that you do better than your supposed best."

Which he did: After moving to the U.S. and gaining citizenship in the 1960s, his fortunes multiplied. Eventually, Jack Kent Cooke owned the Chrysler Building in New York City and, at various times, the Los Angeles Lakers and the Washington Redskins, among other franchise acquisitions. In his lifetime, he had five wives (well four, actually, since he married the same woman twice) and his marriages ranged in duration from 73 days to 45 years. Upon his death in 1997, he left the bulk of his considerable billionaire fortune not to his children, but to a foundation that would serve young people like he once was: incredibly smart, creative, and driven, but from modest economic circumstances. Jack Kent Cooke believed that if you gave high-achieving kids with financial need the proper guidance and resources in high school, college, and beyond, their greatness would emerge. Thus was born the Jack Kent Cooke Foundation (JKCF; see http://www.jkcf.org). Here's how it works.

Launched in 2000, the JKCF now has many program components. Applications for the Young Scholars Program (ironically, the same name as the initial DITD program) are available at the end of seventh grade. Students who are accepted—about 65 students annually—begin their program in eighth grade, continuing on through high school and beyond. Chosen for both their academic and extracurricular accomplishments in athletics or the arts, selected students may attend summer programs for gifted youth, distance learning classes, and specialized music or art instruction, or even receive private school tuition, if no public high school seems appropriate for a particular student's learning. The average applicant's family earns less than $30,000 per year, with 90% of applicants' families earning less than $60,000.

A second program component, the Undergraduate Transfer Scholarship Program provides financial assistance to accomplished community college students who wish to pursue a 4-year degree at a top-tier university. One such student is Linda Rodriguez, a student at Miami-Dade College who is described on the JKCF website. Linda was homeless and jobless at age 17, so her future did not appear bright. However, thanks to a professor at Miami-Dade who recognized Linda's potential, she began school, despite her life obstacles. Two years later, she graduated with a 3.97 GPA while holding down two jobs. Not to mention, she codirected her school's Model United Nations squad. Selected by JKCF for their Transfer Scholarship Program, Linda will earn a B.S. in sociology at Georgetown University, with goals of becoming a lawyer and, later, a judge.

In addition, there is a College Scholarship Program, where awardees receive up to $30,000 annually to attend a 4-year college; the Graduate Arts Award, in which honored students receive up to $50,000 annually to attend an art or music school of their choice; the Good Neighbor Grants, $10,000–$35,000 given to local institutions in the greater Washington, DC, area to support high-poverty kids through activities like tennis, chess, and digital journalism; and the Talent Development Award, the first of which was a $500,000 award given in 2012 to the Renzulli Academy in Hartford, CT—a K–8 school for gifted children from low-income families. This award will allow the Renzulli Academy to expand to three new cities.

With foreign travel encouraged, many of the JKCF Scholars provide essential services globally in the areas of health and education to others who need assistance. And just for good measure, two scholars who first met at an "All Scholars Weekend" in 2006, Jason Stern and Caraleigh Holverson, were married in 2009. Both were transfer students from community colleges and now, with their college careers behind them, Jason is an engineer and Caraleigh is a Truman Scholar, a highly competitive program for individuals who wish to pursue careers in public service. You gotta think that Jack Kent Cooke would take some pride in this union.

In a letter written by a recently arrived immigrant to the U.S. in 1917 to his family back in Europe, comes this sentiment: "Before I came to America, I heard that the streets were paved with gold. When I arrived, I learned three things. First, the streets weren't paved with gold. Second, they weren't paved at all. And third, I was expected to pave them."

The generosity of people like Jack Kent Cooke has made many such pavings possible.

FROM PRISON TO PROMISE

Cody Stothers is a 22-year-old gifted young man who is currently enrolled at Vanderbilt University in a dual Ph.D./ M.D. program. That's a far stretch from his humble beginnings, for, as a recent profile on the student (Wilemon, 2013) noted, Cody was born in a prison hospital in Arkansas just 2 days before Christmas in 1991. A few days later, he was brought home in a Christmas stocking by his grandmother, Frances Taylor, who raised Cody on a disability income of less than $10,000 a year. Always stressing to Cody that an education was the best path out of poverty, Taylor often frequented the library with her grandson—because there, the books were free.

Cody's path to Vanderbilt may have been laid by his grandmother, but another opportunity accelerated his rise. A program called Aspirnaut (http://www.aspirnaut.org) focuses on the STEM areas of science, technology, engineering, and math, and attempts to engage children as young as 5 years old in programs that are rigorous and engaging. Begun by two Vanderbilt professors—one of whom nearly dropped out of high school due to life circumstances—Cody happened to live in a town where the Aspirnaut program existed and he became one of its participants. As he grew, Cody became a tutor for younger kids just learning computer skills. And recently, he and 82 other students coauthored a journal article based on their research in drug therapies to fight cancer.

Cody learned about his acceptance into the dual-doctorate program right around his birthday. The white cake with hefty and colorful decorations that his grandmother had made for his birthday must have tasted sweet, indeed.

. . . AND YET ANOTHER PLAYER

Similar in design to JKCF is the Caroline D. Bradley Scholarship, managed by the not-for-profit Institute for Educational Advancement (IEA; http://www.educationaladvancement.org) based in South Pasadena, CA. (Disclaimer: I am a member of IEA's Board of Directors.) Like JKCF, this scholarship is open to highly gifted seventh graders who exhibit both advanced academic talent and personal excellence. Scholars have been selected each year since 1999, and initially, just California-based students were involved. Today, the pool of active students and alumni is national in composition. In addition to paying the full tuition to any high school that can actualize the individual students' talents, there is also an annual 3-day symposium where present and former Scholars discuss issues of global importance and personal relevance. Their presence is complemented with renowned guest speakers who interact with the Scholars throughout the 3-day event. One distinction between the Bradley scholarship and the JKCF program is that the Bradley Scholarship is need-blind—that is, students from all economic strata are invited to apply. In discussing the impact of the Bradley scholarship, one parent commented, "Doors, opportunities, and experiences opened up to (our son) in ways none of us could ever dream about. He is able to attend a high school that meets all of his individual needs and goals" (IEA, n.d., sidebar).

In addition to the Bradley Scholarship, IEA also sponsors day and residential programs for gifted students in elementary through high school, and organizes the annual Camp Yunasa residential summer programs, a week-long summer camp experience in both Michigan and Colorado for highly gifted children ages 10 and up.

This abundance of private-sector generosity toward gifted children from the foundations highlighted here contrasts vividly with the lack of financial incentives provided by the public sector at either the state or national level. One has to wonder why these governmental agencies do not see the proper education of gifted children as important to our nation's economic and intellectual vitality. Shortsighted thinking may be just the tip of this iceberg of ignorance.

AN ALPHABET SOUP OF OPTIONS

If there is one thing most everyone can agree on, it is that educators are masters of the acronym: PBL, AP, STEM, VA, IB. This propensity to drizzle everything down to an alphabetical mélange may be convenient, but it can also be confusing. Still, the programs and ideas behind these acronyms hold much promise for gifted learners (and others, since none of these options was designed for exclusive use by gifted students), if they are implemented with care and precision. Let's take a look at some of these provisions that, although imperfect, are beneficial options to consider.

PROBLEM-BASED LEARNING (PBL)

Sophomore Tom Wagner's American History class at Simley High School in Inver Grove Heights, MN, had taken its end-of-course exams—but there were still several weeks to go until school was dismissed for the summer. What to do?

In passing, Tom's teacher mentioned in class that a local historic bridge was scheduled for demolition in 2 months. The Rock Island Swing Bridge had been built in 1894 and, having been closed since 1999 due to safety concerns, had reverted to being a hangout for skateboarders and a sightseeing stop for folks wanting a scenic glimpse of the Mississippi River. That's when Tom and his classmates got an idea: They would save the bridge from demolition.

Quickly putting together a community breakfast near the bridge, and advertising about this breakfast via both old-school (church bulletins) and contemporary (Facebook) messaging, the students raised almost $1,000 in their grassroots effort to save the bridge. Attracting the attention of local historic and preservation societies, members of this sophomore class made a presentation to the city council, asking that the bridge be saved and the area turned into a recreational park. The city council passed the proposal, sending their request to the Minnesota state legislature, where it also passed. Governor Tim Pawlenty signed into law a moratorium preventing the bridge's destruction.

Today, the park is a reality, owned and maintained by the city where it rests. Engineers were hired to design and refurbish the bridge and park, and a stone marker near the bridge credits the reason for its continued existence: a sophomore American History class at Simley High School. Tom Wagner's comment? "Saving the bridge was the best thing we ever did" (Branch, 2011, p. 3).

When adults think back on their most engaging learning experiences, they seldom mention the awesome algebra test they took in eighth grade or the over-the-top diorama of the solar system that they made out of Styrofoam balls. No, what they recall—what *we* recall— are those times when our learning ended up mattering to someone more than just us. Such engaging times in school are more rare than common, but when they occur, most students find themselves in the educational equivalent of Nirvana. And when activities like these occur *purposefully*, because teachers and students see their merits, they are practicing a form of education called Problem-Based Learning (PBL).

The PBL movement began at McMaster University in Hamilton, Ontario, in the 1960s. Professors at the university's medical school were seeing their aspiring doctors becoming bored and disillusioned with the medical school curriculum—the memorizing, the testing, the terminology. The plaintive cries of "Is this relevant?" were heard far too often. In response, a different type of education was offered, one that focused on actual medical cases and the dilemmas faced by practicing physicians in trying to treat and cure patients of their maladies. The results were startling . . . in a good way. Students were becoming engaged problem solvers with an eye toward critical thinking and making judgments that actually had consequences.

This type of training was eventually picked up by other medical schools (about 80% of them currently use some elements of PBL) and eventually by schools of law, education, and other domains where real-world simulations turned out to be incredible learning tools.

In the 1990s, the PBL idea made it into middle and high schools (at least in *some* of them), and quite a few programs for gifted students adopted a PBL approach to teaching and learning. As you might imagine, the fundamental roles of teacher and student change drastically in using PBL. For example, the teacher is not the disseminator of everything important (the "sage on the stage") but becomes, instead, the "guide on the side"—the individual who puts out fuzzy problems for the students to examine, tease apart, and attempt to solve. Students in PBL are no longer the stay-in-your-seat recipients of lecture after lecture. Instead, they gain knowledge of a particular topic through reading, research, discussion, and using collaboration with other students to put their problem-solving skills to work—just as Tom Wagner did in Minnesota. PBL uses the following guiding principles:

◇ What do we know already about the topic?

◇ What do we want or need to find out about our topic?

◇ How will we go about finding answers or solutions, and who can best help us do that?

If this sounds like real-world problem solving to you—that's because it is. And although PBL was not designed for exclusive use with gifted students, it's not a big leap to see how the innate curiosity of many gifted kids, coupled with their desire to be self-directed and to think in integrative ways, would attract gifted students like a magnet grabs metal. The work of gifted advocate Shelagh Gallagher on PBL units of study is extensive, as she has written units on topics such as the Black Death, endangered species, and Chinese immigration into the U.S. Further, Joyce VanTassel-Baska and her colleagues at the Center for Gifted Education at The College of William and Mary, where VanTassel-Baska was the former director, have constructed dozens of K–12 units in all curriculum areas that use a PBL approach. Too, there are many national competitions that use a PBL approach (or a hybrid of it) to engage students—think Future Problem Solving, National

History Day, or ideas from Edutopia—the educational foundation begun by George Lucas.

In addition to these specific programs, there is now a network of high schools in 24 states involved in the New Tech Network (http://www.newtechnetwork.org). In each of these schools, instruction is based around these outcomes:

◇ content standards,
◇ critical thinking,
◇ oral and written communication,
◇ career preparation,
◇ citizenship and ethics, and
◇ technology literacy.

These skills are imbedded in student projects and assessments, as well as being indicators of growth on student grade reports. Does New Tech work? Well, at New Tech High School in Napa, CA, which has been instructing students in this manner since 1996, 98% of students graduate and 95% enroll in postsecondary schools, as compared to less than 40% for other Napa Valley high schools. And, 40% of its graduates enter into a science- or math-focused career path, as opposed to 7% nationally. It's hard to argue with stats like these! Also, name a high school student who would not like to be under contract with NASA to develop sports that astronauts can play on the moon for exercise—just one of New Tech's many PBL-based learning opportunities.

If there is any criticism of PBL, it is one with which many gifted advocates can live with: the "cognitive load" is often too much for some students to absorb. In other words, when you are examining an adult topic (say, the aforementioned Chinese immigration issue or the astronauts' free-time games), you are not only confronted with facts and figures, but prejudices, morals, economic and political consequences, etc. In order to succeed and to respect the enormity of the topic and subtopics you'll discover, you'll need many skills that are not required when memorizing multiplication tables: organization, time management, an ability to distinguish the important from the trivial. These skills are seldom innate and they do need practice to master. However, a careful, competent teacher can "scaffold" students' learning experiences in PBL so that the topic or task does not become completely overwhelming. And the materials available from Gallagher, the Center for Gifted Education, and others will be good guides in providing such assistance, as will the exemplar schools available through the New Tech Network.

The bottom line is this: if you are looking for a mode of teaching and learning that has proven itself effective in times that matter most—like in the surgical suite or in a Supreme Court chamber—you should give PBL a thorough look-see.

THE STEM INITIATIVE

America Online (AOL) cofounder Steve Case, in trying to get the U.S. Congress to pass the Startup Act 2.0, a bill that improves the environment for entrepreneurs to create and expand businesses, cited these remarkable statistics in a 2012 article: "More than 40% of Fortune 500 companies were founded by immigrants or their children, and they employ over 10 million individuals . . . IBM, Google and Apple were founded by an immigrant or the child of an immigrant" (p. 1).

As of this writing, the Startup Act 2.0 bill is still languishing in the political mire of Capitol Hill, but the justification behind its importance is obvious to educators and business people alike: If the next generation of entrepreneurs and societal change-agents is to emerge from our K–12 schools and colleges, it'll happen by design, not happenstance.

Enter STEM education. Even noneducators seem to know the scenario: When America's kids are stacked up against kids in other countries in science and math success . . . well, America's kids don't stack up so highly. The reasons for these less-than-stellar statistics are the cause celebres of many organizations, including the Organization for Economic Cooperation and Development (OECD). In its 2011 annual report, OECD found that among 42 nations analyzed, the U.S. ranks 14th in the percentage of college graduates, 36th in high school graduation rates, and 26th in the percentage of 4-year-olds in early childhood education programs (OECD, 2012). With these data behind them and chagrined by what seems like a steady decline in America's educational prowess, folks from all walks of life—school, business, government—began advocating in the early years of the new millennium for what had been languishing in many U.S. classrooms: an emphasis on high-level instruction in the areas of science (S), technology (T), engineering (E), and mathematics (M). Somewhat reminiscent of the Sputnik scare of the mid-1950s, when science and math in schools took off like the rocket that Sputnik was, hand-wringing adults are now calling for a new focus on STEM instruction. Whereas the argument in the 1950s was one of national security—the Russians are our enemies and we need to beat them—the argument of 2013 is one of economics: the Chinese are our competitors and we need to beat them. Same tune, different key.

The principles behind STEM instruction, from elementary school through college, will sound familiar to many of the other trends reviewed in this book: to help students gain skills required to succeed in today's challenging world—the ability to think critically, to solve complex problems, and to drive advancements in STEM-focused fields. Good for all students, to be sure, but almost mandatory when it comes to gifted students' educations.

Between the U.S. Departments of Education and Labor, as well as the infusion of monies from companies that have a vested interest in the STEM arena (e.g., Intel, Target, Cisco, and IBM, each of which has invested more than $1 billion in STEM projects), tens of billions of dollars are pouring into programs that will prepare students for the 80% of future jobs that will require some STEM experience (Schiller & Arena, 2012). Even former Los Angeles Laker Kareem Abdul-Jabbar is in on the STEM scene, as he was named a STEM Ambassador by the state of California in 2012, traveling the state trying to convince others of the need to begin afterschool STEM-related programs.

It is still too early to tell if the flood of STEM efforts will have a dramatic positive effect on the education of our nation's children or if, like Sputnik, the movement will peter out when the next best thing comes along. Certainly, the focus on STEM's high-level, hands-on, career-focused goals will attract the minds of many a gifted youngster . . . but not all. What about our future wordsmiths and artists? Are their needs and strengths to be ignored, sidetracked, or minimized on behalf of STEM? The Americans for the Arts (http://www. artsusa.org) advocacy group hopes not. They propose changing STEM to STEAM, where the "A" inclusion adds in the important arts component. Thinking critically, integrating disciplines, and refining cognitive and creative skills—aren't these elements embedded within arts instruction, too?

And just to quell the Chicken Littles among us who think that the sky is, indeed, falling and that America's kids are on track to be deadbeat losers when it comes to global competition, Gregory Ferenstein (2012), a critic of some of these international school comparisons, reminds us of these facts: Since international comparisons began in 1964, the United States has *never* led the pack. In America, we educate *every* child, not just the elite few, and unlike more linguistically pure nations like Korea or Japan or Estonia, the United States has countless languages spoken throughout the thousands of schools dotting our land. And even though kids in Chinese schools have twice as many instructional days a year as do students in the U.S., both nations have *identical scores* on tests of scientific reasoning.

To be sure, the United States needs to prop up its educational standards for any child for whom the bar is set too low, but when you consider that 17% of all international college students in the world come to American universities, and that we remain the global leader in both economics and innovation, Chicken Little's fears of educational annihilation might be a bit overblown.

Still, programs like STEM and PBL are not widespread in our nation's schools, and it would be rare to find a primary or elementary school where the skills needed to succeed in a STEM or PBL high school environment are taught purposefully. Too many teachers and administrators, beholden to the almighty test that proves whether a school is worthwhile, cling to practices where the main criterion for success seems to be how accurately a student can fill in the appropriate circle on a test of basic comprehension. We have a long way to go before we can, as a nation, claim victory over educational malpractice.

OH, SAY CAN YOU SEE?

Generally speaking, enrichment programs for gifted students are limited to the elementary school years. However, in eastern Pennsylvania, Intermediate Unit 13, a year-long series of one-day seminars for gifted middle and high school students has operated since 1982. Called "SEE (Student Enrichment Experiences) Seminars," each day-long experience introduces students to experts and professionals in a variety of fields. Each SEE Seminar offers a topic not typically available in classrooms, exposing students to a wide variety of highly engaging experiences. Some of the more than thirty 2013–2014 SEE Seminars for middle school gifted students included wilderness survival, career exploration, human anatomy, and African dance and culture, while some of the high school options ranged from watchmaking, to community involvement and enhancement, to the physics of flight, to brain anatomy. The SEE seminars can be a part of a gifted student's "GEP" (Gifted Education Plan), a state-mandated document that is required for every identified gifted student in Pennsylvania. Focusing on creativity, originality, problem solving, and complex and sophisticated content, the SEE seminar participants realize the benefit of these services, as noted in these student comments on the program's website:

◇ *"I will be able to use what I learned about flying in different aspects of engineering."*

◇ *"You are surrounded by other smart people, and the person teaching you knows you are smart, so they make it challenging."*

◇ *"A SEE Seminar is a more immersive method of teaching. I am willing to learn about a topic I am actually interested in."*

Secondary-level students need more than just harder content in high school classes—they also need to experience the world beyond high school. SEE Seminars are just one innovative way to expose gifted students to the world beyond

*their school's walls. More information can be found at http://
www.iu13.org/EducatorsandAdministrators/Pages/Gifted
EducationPrograms.aspx.*

VIRTUAL ACADEMIES (VA)

Ever since I was a little boy, I've been an early riser. Even on
Saturdays, when cartoon watching was my morning staple, I began
my TV time at 6:30 a.m. There weren't any cartoons on at that hour,
but there was something better: a guy named Jon Gnagy who was
going to teach me how to draw. When switching channels during the
commercials (which, of course, urged me to buy his drawing kit), I
often found what looked like a schoolroom with adults sitting in it.
Indeed, it was. It was a college-level class on some complicated subject
with a guy wearing a necktie giving a lecture. Little did I know at the
time that these two shows were harbingers of what was to occur a
generation later: virtual learning. What was old is new.

Although virtual schools are available to kids in all grade levels
at an ever-increasing rate (some would say an *alarming* rate), they are
not a new idea. The first one appeared in 1929. That was when some
forward-thinkers at the University of Nebraska began the Independent
Study High School (ISHS), a real bricks-and-mortar school for kids
who may never have attended it in person. Remember, Nebraska is a
rural state that covers 77,420 square miles—that's a lot of geography.
So with many high school students attending very small schools
in isolated pockets of the Cornhusker state, there weren't many
opportunities for advanced-level courses. How could a school that
graduates 20 kids a year possibly offer calculus or British Literature?
And even if there were a bunch of teens ready to tackle *Paradise Lost* in
Beaver City, NE (population: 636), would there would be any teacher
in town knowledgeable and qualified enough to teach the course?

What ISHS did in 1929 was to provide advanced courses for
high school students who earned their academic credits through
correspondence. That's right, learning materials and tests would be sent
by mail from ISHS faculty to a sponsor (usually a teacher) in whichever
high school one or more students were enrolled in a particular course.

The ISHS faculty would then have the assignments and tests returned to them for grading. When students passed the course, they then earned high school credit. It was possible in 1929 to earn a high school diploma at ISHS without ever stepping foot on its campus. Today, it still is.

Obviously, technology has enabled ISHS to offer its courses online (see http://www.highschool.unl.edu). Currently, it serves thousands of students from all 50 states and 135 nations. It is an accredited high school, so its diploma is recognized by nearly all universities. Students not only get course instruction, they also get academic advising. The student body is incredibly diverse, even including world-class athletes and performers whose schedules don't allow them to attend a local high school on a full-time basis.

The ISHS may have been a groundbreaking idea in 1929 but today, it is just one of 150+ VAs nationwide. Virtually every state (excuse the pun) has at least one VA—like Alabama—and more populous states like Ohio and California have 30+ VAs within their borders. (It's hard to provide an accurate count of the actual number of VAs, as new ones are added on a constant basis.) Some of the VAs are funded with public school monies, so that the dollars that would typically go to the brick-and-mortar elementary school down your block now gets shifted to the VA's coffers. Other VAs are for-profit institutions that may or may not be funded with public monies (a legislative decision made at the state level). The largest conglomerate of for-profit VAs is called K12, Inc., a publicly traded company that manages schools in many states. One school managed by K12, Inc, Agora Academy, had an enrollment of 8,800 students in the 2010–2011 school year, receiving an average of $5,500–$6,000 of public money *per student, each year* (Saul, 2011). With such an abundant war chest of available funds, you'd think that achievement would be high, right? Well, in a comprehensive analysis of Agora's test results, Saul (2011) reported that only one-third of the 8,800 students had reached Annual Yearly Progress (AYP), a federally imposed benchmark used to determine whether a student is learning as much as expected in a year's time.

As you might imagine, it's not hard to find criticism of VAs, especially those that are run for profit. In addition to the low rate of student success that is not uncommon in VAs, there is a substantial "churn rate" (the number of student withdrawals annually), accusations that teachers are overworked with too many students (and underpaid, to boot), and still more accusations that it is sometimes impossible to determine if the virtual student is doing the actual work. Also, if a VA accepts any public funds, it does not have a choice as to whether to accept a student. So if a student is not self-motivated and the parent is not willing to invest considerable time in this virtual education, the likelihood of success seems minimal.

However, proponents of VAs will point out that the flexibility afforded to students who *are* self-motivated is reason enough to applaud the presence of VAs. So if you have a gifted student who can whiz through curriculum quickly and accurately, a VA lets him progress at his own pace. And, at many virtual high schools—Stanford University's Online High School and the University of Missouri and University of Oklahoma high schools, to name three, students can be dual enrolled in high school and college classes, with one virtual course awarding credit toward both a high school diploma and a college degree. Something else to consider: If your VA is not funded by public dollars, the costs can be steep. For example, a full-year tuition at Stanford Online High School was $16,600 in 2014, with part-time enrollment (up to three courses) costing $10,300. One might be wise to ask if the "Stanford" logo on your sheepskin is worth that annual expense if other less costly options are nearby.

The best candidate for attending a VA is a self-starter who does not need to be prodded constantly to keep up with lessons. After all, isn't it human nature to take the path of least resistance when you can? This attitude doesn't work well in a *typical* school, but it'll be academically lethal in a virtual one. In addition, parents need to make sure that the VA they are considering for their child be regionally or nationally accredited. This is especially vital at the high school level, as your child doesn't want to be awarded a diploma that her college of choice doesn't recognize as valid. Also, keeping gifted students in mind, make sure the VA you are looking at has AP options (and teachers qualified to teach these courses), college-level classes beyond AP, and a variety of elective options in more esoteric areas like Latin or aviation science or journalism. It's a buyer's market out there with VAs. *Caveat emptor* is definitely in order.

The latest wrinkle in virtual education is called a MOOC—*M*assive *O*pen *O*nline *C*ourse. One web-based platform, called edX, provides courses from elite universities to a global audience—for free. Launched in 2012 by Harvard University and the Massachusetts Institute of Technology (MIT), edX hosts MOOCs from these two universities as well as from Georgetown University, Wellesley College, the University of Texas, and the University of California, Berkeley. Already, it has 500,000+ worldwide users. A competing MOOC platform, Coursera, hosts classes by other universities like Johns Hopkins University, the Universities of Maryland and Virginia, and more than 30 other institutions of higher education. Even larger than edX, Coursera has more than 2 million participants. The folks who run edX and Coursera are very selective in which places they accept—hundreds of universities apply, but few are chosen.

With MOOCs, each university selects courses in its areas of noted strength—for example, Georgetown University offers MOOCs in international relations, law, and public policy. As of now, no university is awarding academic credit for taking a MOOC, although folks at both the nonprofit edX and the for-profit Coursera admit to looking for ways to generate revenue without charging tuition. Until then, students who take MOOCs are learning for the sake of learning—what a concept!

Expect to hear much more about MOOCs in the coming years. Who knows? Someday your child may be able to earn college credit at Harvard and Georgetown simultaneously without ever having been to either institution.

John Gnagy and that necktie-wearing Saturday morning professor must be proud of what they started!

ADVANCED PLACEMENT (AP)

One of the benchmarks by which successful high schools are measured is how many Advanced Placement courses are offered and what percentage of students score well enough on the year-end AP exams to earn college credit for their efforts.

> The best thing anyone can do for the psyche of a gifted child is to place him or her in the company of other gifted children. Oftentimes, an intelligent child may value independence over almost anything else. But while logging in some "me time" may be important to them, it's just as likely that they feel alienated from their current peers. Gifted children are like plants that grow more effectively when together. (But feel free to come up with a better metaphor for the gifted children in your life than "you're a plant!")
>
> *Alec Bojalad, former gifted child,*
> *current recovering college graduate, Twinsburg, OH*

Advanced Placement classes began in 1955, after a 3-year study at elite private high schools and colleges showed that high school seniors were capable of handling college course content. Administered by the College Board, AP courses are now available in the majority of America's high schools in 35 different subject areas, from U.S. History (the most frequently offered course) to more esoteric courses such as Statistics, Human Geography, and Studio Art: 3D Design. The larger the high school, the more AP courses it is likely to offer to students.

Advanced Placement courses are designed to offer more rigorous course content and often have the extra advantage of being taught by a school's most qualified teachers. Too, class sizes tend to be smaller and discipline problems less common than in non-AP courses. The courses' content is created by a panel of subject-area experts and college professors of the respective disciplines covered by the particular AP courses. Prescriptive by design, AP course content is uniform from one school to the next. This is of vital importance to the integrity of AP, as students are invited to take standardized AP tests at the end of each course (currently, $87 per test) to determine if they score well enough to earn college credits. Each test is scored on a 5-point scale; universities do not grant credit for scores of 1 or 2, while a score of 3 or 4 may or may not qualify. An AP test score of 5 is almost always given credit by the accepting college. Nearly 90% of higher education institutions have policies regarding AP grading credit, so it is a ubiquitous program that finds several million students participating annually.

On its surface, the AP agenda looks perfect for those gifted students for whom high achievement is important. Not only does the gifted student have a high school course that will be challenging in content, but the prospect of earning college credit while still in high school is alluring—especially to parents, who are looking at the tuition money saved if their son or daughter can enter college with even a few classes already paid for by AP credits. So because the original goal of AP was to place students appropriately in college classes based on their extant knowledge base, it is doing its job.

With, of course, some caveats.

In a book published in 2010, *Advanced Placement: A Critical Examination of the Advanced Placement Program*, Sadler, Sonnert, Tai, and Klopfenstein criticized AP, "the juggernaut of American high school education" (p. 3), for several reasons. First, the authors found that students who took AP courses in the sciences but failed the AP exam performed no better in college than students without any AP courses at all. Further, college professors who teach students in advanced college courses where students were "excused" from entry-level courses due to getting a score of 3 or 4 on their AP tests frequently reported that these students are not prepared for the content of the more advanced college courses. From the perspective of AP saving money and time for students in college, this critical examination found no evidence of this claim's validity. Students stay just as long in college; they merely take other courses.

The authors of *Advanced Placement: A Critical Examination of the Advanced Placement Program* pointed to other concerns as well (most of which deal with issues of equity), including one that can also affect the learning of gifted students. Specifically, the authors contend that because most high schools do not restrict entrance into AP courses, any student who wishes to enroll has the opportunity (and the right) to do so. Although this sounds equitable, one must ask if the depth of course content, or the pace of instruction, must be lowered to accommodate the learning needs of those students not prepared for AP's rigor. This situation of equity has economic costs, too. For example, in a 2006 study (Jaschik, 2010) in California, $2.8 million in federal funds was awarded to subsidize AP exam costs for those unable to pay the $87 test exam fee. With 41% of the students taking the exam failing to get even a score of 3, $1.1 million was spent on students who ultimately failed to achieve their goal.

Patrick Welsh (2009), an English teacher in Virginia and a frequent critic of the AP program, called AP a "game of labels and numbers, a public relations ploy used by school officials who are dumping as many students as they can into A.P. courses to create the illusion that they are raising overall standards" (para. 2). Welsh further contended that AP courses do not increase the number of low-income or minority students attending college, confirming what other critics have noted—that the majority of students who take AP courses are college bound to begin with. Welsh further criticized AP's contention that taking such courses raises standards in the high schools where the courses are offered or decreases the achievement gap between wealthy White students and other students. His solution? Drop the AP label and simply provide a detailed description of the course and the workload demanded by those who take it. Then, for students who take the challenge, they can still take the AP exam at year's end (yes, taking an AP course *is not* a prerequisite for taking an AP exam).

Several schools and school districts have done exactly that. For example, in a bold move that infuriated some parents, the school board in Scarsdale, NY—a wealthy enclave with outstanding schools and high-achieving students—eliminated all AP courses in 2008 and replaced them with courses they termed "Advanced Topics." These new courses would be the most rigorous offered at Scarsdale High School, and they would offer in-depth analysis of particular subjects instead of the fact-based regimen that is often associated with AP courses. Prior to implementing this change, school superintendent Michael McGill said he wanted to "empower our graduates to rise to the challenges of the 21st century" (Scharfenberg, 2007, p. 1). The Advanced Topics alternative is still in effect in Scarsdale and parental fears of students being unable to get into exclusive colleges and universities without AP credits have gone unfounded, as the Advanced Topics courses are thoroughly described on each high school transcript. Also, students are encouraged to take AP tests each May, and in the 2010–2011 school year, more than 96% of students who did so earned AP scores high enough to earn college credits. This implicit criticism of AP courses, combined with an inquiry-based set of advanced classes as an alternative, may be a model that other schools wish to consider as a way to serve their most capable high school students. High Tech High in San Diego and Cranbrook Kingswood School in Michigan (among others) have done just that.

Despite these exceptions and the valid criticisms leveled at AP, most anyone working in secondary education today would bet against AP fully losing its allure and decreasing substantially in popularity. In fact, if recent numbers continue, the estimated 25% of high school students who took at least one AP test in 2010 is likely to surge higher in years ahead.

The bottom line is this: When AP courses are taught by highly qualified teachers, and the enrolled students are surrounded by at least some classmates who are equally adept and anxious to learn, their benefits are many. However, for students who prefer a different kind of rigor, one that offers a much broader, more analytical view of education as a whole, the Advanced Topics option likely holds more allure. Or better still, these inquisitive students might opt for a comprehensive option that may be a better fit: the International Baccalaureate program.

THE INTERNATIONAL BACCALAUREATE (IB) PROGRAM

Sometimes, the best ideas emerge from strife. In the case of the IB program, that is exactly the case. Following World War II, a woman named Marie-Therese Maurette was commissioned by UNESCO to write a handbook on how educators could help their students to become more globally aware and socially conscious. Her 1948 publication, "Is There a Way of Teaching for Peace?" was the genesis of a movement that continues to this day: the IB Diploma Programme.

It did take more than a decade for Maurette's work to make it into mainstream schools via IB. That's when a group of teachers at the International School of Geneva decided to plan a course of study for students ages 16–19 whose families moved frequently. This Diploma Programme had the goal of providing an internationally acceptable university admission qualification for the growing number of students whose parents were part of the world of diplomacy or who worked for international and multinational organizations. Essentially, by designing a curriculum that would be the same in international schools wherever they were located—from Australia to Zanzibar—students who changed schools frequently would be able to pick up, academically speaking, where they left off at their previous school. These standardized courses and assessments began in Europe (IB's international headquarters has been in Geneva, Switzerland, since 1968), making it to the United States in 1975.

At its inception, IB was focused entirely on high school age populations. Then, in the mid-1990s, a Middle Years Programme (MYP) began, followed in 1996 by PYP, the Primary Years Programme. Today, the IB programme encompasses children from 146 nations, from ages 3–19, in both independent and public school settings.

Although IB should not be construed as a gifted program, the elements that make up its curriculum and the types of assessments required from the students make it a very good match, indeed, for highly intelligent children. Let's consider some of IB's hallmarks.

The pedagogical foundation of the IB Diploma Programme for high school students is called TOK or Theory of Knowledge, a compulsory course that introduces students to the various ways people learn—through their senses, through reasoning, through perception, and through emotion. These avenues of learning are explored through the typical disciplines found in most high schools—natural and human sciences, mathematics, the arts, languages, and ethics. A culminating experience, the "Extended Essay," is an independent, self-directed research paper of approximately 4,000 words. This essay must emphasize communicating information and/or developing an argument that uses analysis, synthesis, and evaluation in its construction. Students self-select a topic in any of eight general topic areas—English, foreign language, history, business, science, film, etc.— and are assisted along the way by a supervisor (often, a teacher at the student's school). Approximately 40–50 hours of work are expected to complete the Extended Essay and, at its conclusion, the essay is evaluated by representatives of the IB organization on a 0–36 point scale, judging everything from the legitimacy of the research question, to the means of analyzing the question, to the final presentation of the document. Recent Extended Essays in the area of history have focused on such diverse topics as "Gandhi in South Africa" to "Lenin's Genius" to "Women in the 1960s." The overall goal of the Extended Essay is to prepare students for research they might conduct when they enter universities.

In 2012, IB added a new component to its program, a "career-related certificate," which opens up participation to 16- to 19-year-old students who are engaged in learning that makes a positive difference to future lives. Career competencies and lifelong learning are stressed.

The Middle Years Programme uses the same eight core subject areas as its high school counterpart, emphasizing both holistic learning and intercultural awareness. Embedded within the curriculum are themes like these: community and service, human ingenuity, health and social education, and approaches to learning. A culminating project ends the MYP and serves as a springboard to students going ahead to the Diploma Programme in high school.

Finally, the Primary Years Program uses six transdisciplinary themes to engage young students in big thinking: "Who we are," "How we express ourselves," "How we organize ourselves," "Where we are in place and time", "How the world works," and "Sharing the planet." Under these broad-based categories, it's hard to imagine anything less than integrated teaching and learning, something that even young gifted children want when they ask questions in school like "When am I ever going to need this?" In the IB program offerings, from PYP through the Diploma Programme, this essential question is answered time after time.

The IB Mission Statement notes that IB is designed to "develop inquiring, knowledgeable and caring young people who help to create a better and more peaceful world through intercultural understanding and respect" (IB, n.d., para. 5). As you can imagine, this global focus does have its critics, as some have accused it of being Marxist, foreign, globalist, and anti-American. For example, Margaret Dayton, a Utah state senator, voted in 2008 to cut the IB budget by two-thirds. As Dayton wrote, "I don't want to create 'world citizens' nearly as much as I want to help cultivate American citizens who function well in the world . . . the IB program teaches a skeptical, unattached philosophy of world citizenship . . . it is not governed by Americans" (p. 1).

Another critic, Lisa McLoughlin, who manages a website titled truthaboutib.com, takes issue with the high cost of starting and operating an IB program. Indeed, between the IB application fee, teacher training fees (all IB teachers are required to have specialized training, unlike AP teachers), and the on-site evaluation done by IB personnel, costs can run into the $50,000+ range to implement the program. However, *Washington Post* education writer Jay Mathews, a proponent of both AP and IB, finds that IB is preferable to AP for both its broadly based, thematic instruction and its integrated curriculum offerings. And, when considering the $56,000 cost for his local high school to implement IB, Mathews noted that this cost is about the same amount paid to operate this high school's baseball and softball teams. As he wrote, "as much as I adore these sports, which my children played, I think IB is more important" (Mathews, 2010, para. 19).

The final criticism—and an important one—is that many colleges and universities aren't sure what to do when a matriculating student walks in with an IB diploma. In what subjects do they get credit for the work they have done? With AP, discrete courses can be sidestepped by matching the AP American History course with a freshman-level college course of the same name. With IB, this direct linkage is not clear. When this occurs, it will be incumbent on the incoming IB graduate to meet with both admission officials and individual professors to make sure he is placed in appropriately challenging courses, especially early on in the college career.

Despite these criticisms, IB (from my biased perspective) has a great deal of good to offer many students, but especially gifted ones. Our gifted kids are the ones who think globally *naturally*, as they marry disparate ideas to each other and can see the connections between literature, history, and music. In IB, such integration and overlap of subject matter is expected *and* respected.

HOMESCHOOLING GIFTED CHILDREN

Universal public education in America was a mid-19th century invention. Prior to then, formal instruction in schools was limited to those who could afford to pay for their kids to be tutored and taught. For the masses, their education was often limited in content, depth, and duration. Call it homeschooling by default.

So when the homeschooling movement became increasingly popular in the 1980s, the societal backlash surprised many. Why would parents willingly give up the hard-earned right for their kids to receive a free public education and, instead, teach them at home? Were these parents those who lived on society's fringes, wishing to inculcate in their children sets of moral or religious beliefs that would bring extremism or anarchy to our country?

Well, perhaps for a tiny amount of homeschooling parents, anarchy was their goal. But for most, the reasons fell into one of three camps: (a) the desire to teach their children in a climate more conducive to learning than one that focused so much on student discipline; (b) the wish to include religious and moral instruction into their kids' educational repertoire; or (c) the belief that the school curriculum was too rigid and/or easy, leaving the child bored and unsatisfied. It is in this third camp where homeschooling gifted children resides.

Kathi Kearney, a prominent gifted education specialist with a laser-like focus on meeting the needs of profoundly gifted children, found that even though some parents of gifted kids homeschool them out of *dissatisfaction* with public school offerings, many others do so from a more *positive* position: "homeschooling allows the ideal educational program for a highly gifted child to unfold by providing maximum flexibility" (Kearney, 1992, p. 16). And Kathryn Finn, who initially did not see her children as gifted, just different, entered the homeschooling world because of others in her life—doctors, some teachers, neighbors—who helped her to see that her children's actions and reactions to learning were *natural* reactions to an *unnatural* fit. As Finn (2007) wrote, "(the gifted label) made some of what we had been living with more understandable. And it gave me permission to do things that I wouldn't have otherwise considered" (p. 182).

Even though many parents of gifted children would like the autonomy to steer their kids' minds in directions that are personally meaningful to them, Beverly Hernandez (2012) wrote about some stark realities to confront in making the homeschooling decision:

◇ Do you, as a parent, have the *temperament* to be your child's teacher?

◇ Do you, as a parent, have the *time* and *financial ability* to make homeschooling work?

◇ If there are two parents in the household, do they both agree that homeschooling is a good option?

◇ Does your child believe homeschooling is worth a shot?

These questions are faced by virtually any prospective homeschooling parent, but the next one applies most specifically to parents of gifted kids:

◇ Am I smart enough to teach my own gifted kid?

Ah, yes, the intellectual intimidation factor! Sure, most any mom or dad will be fine with spelling lists and simple addition, but what happens when your child's interests and strengths are in topics you know nothing about? Finn (2007) had an answer for that: See yourself not as the staff, but as the administration, of your child's homeschool. Others around you—college professors, librarians, community members, Scout leaders, church elders, other homeschooling parents— they will be your child's new "teachers," crisscrossing their lives as the needs arise. It's also not unusual (especially in adolescence) for some homeschooled kids to attend a "regular" school on a part-time basis— either their local high school, a community college, or a virtual high school. We all have our limits, intellectually speaking, but being afraid to teach your child's mind shouldn't stifle your desire to give it a try. Homeschooling might be a better fit than you think.

Of course, homeschooling has its critics, including the National Education Association (NEA) which first passed a resolution in 1988 against homeschooling, reiterating their position in 2011 with

Resolution B-82, which reads in part, "The National Education Association believes that home schooling programs based on parental choice cannot provide the student with a comprehensive education experience" (Illinois Review, 2011, p. 1). Of course, those are fightin' words to homeschool advocates, who believe that a broad NEA brushstroke cannot be applied to all children equally. However, the homeschooling parade has passed the NEA by, as now virtually every state has particular rules and regulations regarding homeschooling practices. Some states require annual achievement tests for homeschoolers, others do not. Some states want parents to submit their educational plans for their homeschooler, others do not.

One thing is certain, though: With homeschooling graduates now attending more than 900 higher education institutions, this trend toward student/parent autonomy is unlikely to subside soon. And, with the advent of more virtual schools than ever before coming online, the array of homeschooling options will surely increase in the years ahead.

AND IN THE END

Since I entered the gifted child education field in 1978, I have always been surprised at how vast it is and how many tentacles it has. Not only are gifted advocates concerned about what happens within gifted programs, but they are also keenly aware that not every regular classroom teacher is knowledgeable about how to work effectively with gifted students. Also, the appropriateness of options that should benefit gifted kids but are not the exclusive bastion of gifted child educators—AP courses and IB programs, for example—are of concern to both parents and educators. The social and emotional health of gifted students, over and above the typical concerns in these areas for any child, is another dimension that takes on huge importance when statistics are cited for the number of high school dropouts who are gifted . . . or the number of suicides among gifted youth . . . or the horrifying results of "psychological autopsies" that show the high intellects of many of our nation's worst mass murderers at Columbine, Newtown, Aurora, and other sites that will forever be etched into our memory by the mere mention of the town or school's name.

The needs don't stop there. One must also consider the topic of career guidance for gifted teens who are capable in and passionate about so many occupations; the appropriateness of acceleration, whether it be for a 4-year-old attending kindergarten or a 15-year-old beginning college; and the sociological issues that arise when one considers whether gifted kids, by reason of the great abilities they have, are obligated to give more back to society than a person of average intelligence.

Naively, in 1978, I described gifted child education as being like an octopus, with a limited number of tentacles that reached out to other areas. Today, more than a generation later, I find a more appropriate analogy to be that of a millipede. Yes, it is that broad a field.

As explained in this chapter, the history of our field is a legacy that goes back centuries, not decades. Even if the word "gifted" wasn't used before the early 20th century to describe our world's most capable children, there has been a fascination with high intellect since humanity's onset. And, despite the critics who see gifted child education as being (at best) superfluous and (at worst) undemocratic, the children and adults who receive appropriate educational and psychological support for their intense abilities know the lifelong impact such attention can produce. It is the difference between living life well and living life fully.

Now, if only we can gain the positive attention of political and educational stakeholders who feel otherwise, we may be able to reverse the current war on America's most capable youth.

On to those critics . . .

CHAPTER 3

THE BATTLE OF EQUITY OVER EXCELLENCE

"I Have No Time to Visit With King Arthur"
Kalli Dakos (1995, p. 47)

I have no time to dream a dream
Or think a splendid thought,
Or visit with King Arthur
In the land of Camelot.

I've underlined one hundred nouns
And circled thirty verbs
While wishing that this workbook
Had a story to its words.

I could travel to another time
With Huck Finn on his raft
Or read a poem by Silverstein
That really makes me laugh.

Instead I fill in compound words,
A never-ending chore.

How I long to be with Gulliver
On a strange and distant shore.

Nouns and verbs and compound words
Are sad and dull and stale,
Unless they're fired with the spark
Of a mighty, wondrous tale.

Liam Goodowens is a 6-year-old from Florida who does gymnastics and is learning hip-hop dancing. Rounding out his musical repertoire, Liam enjoys attending rock concerts with his dad. Also, Liam's IQ is in the top 2% of the population but, since his school district offers few services for gifted children, Liam is placed in a regular classroom where he often sits and waits for his classmates to catch up to the teacher's directions. His mom, Samantha, noted the irony: "We are terrified of the average student being 'left behind,' and yet, our brightest children are expected to stay behind" (White, 2012, p. 1).

Liam is just one of countless thousands (millions?) of school-age gifted children whose capabilities are being systematically and callously ignored in deference to a climate that promotes adequacy over excellence. Only an ignorant person would claim that all people are identical in intellect, temperament, or capabilities, yet if you took a long look at many of today's classrooms, you'd see that that is exactly how gifted children are treated.

How did we get to the point where the children in our schools most capable of high achievement and personal growth are the same children whose needs are most neglected decade after decade? Who among the intellectual elite decided that a one-size-fits-all approach to education is appropriate—and why do we listen to these flat-Earthers? When did the tide turn in our educational philosophies and practices so that instead of reaching out to gifted children and giving them a boost up, we squelch their abilities by having them underline nouns and verbs instead of seeking out King Arthur or Huck Finn?

In the words of that great philosopher, Pogo, "We have met the enemy and he is us."

In the following four chapters, I will present related and overarching themes that have gotten us to the sad place we are today vis-à-vis our gifted children and their appropriate education. The themes include:

1. The battle of equity over excellence
2. Interpreting giftedness as "something you do" instead of someone you are"
3. Instructional panaceas that aren't
4. Legislative absurdity

Let's begin with the head of the serpent.

EDUCATING GIFTED CHILDREN: UNNECESSARY HURDLES

In 1961, John W. Gardner wrote one of the greatest tributes to intellectualism: *Excellence: Can We Be Equal and Excellent Too?* Extremely accomplished himself, Gardner served as President of the Carnegie Corporation and as Secretary of Health, Education and Welfare under President Lyndon Johnson. He also received the presidential Medal of Honor, the highest civilian honor bestowed by the U.S. government. No slouch, this guy!

In putting together his book and remarking on the apparent dichotomy between "the two E's"—equity and excellence—Gardner (1961) noted that a book like his "must raise some questions which Americans have shown little inclination to discuss rationally" (p. xi). More than half a century later, such rational discussion still seems lacking.

Why was the discussion needed, both then and now? Here's how Gardner explained it:

> Extreme equalitarianism—or as I would prefer to say, *equalitarianism wrongly conceived*—which ignores differences in native capacity and achievement, has not served democracy well. Carried far enough,

> it means the lopping off of any heads which come above dead level. It means committee rule, the individual smothered by the group. And it means the end of that striving for excellence which has produced mankind's greatest achievements. (pp. 14–15)

Using this logic as his foundation, and using our nation's democratic ideals as the raison d'être to pursue excellence, Gardner went on to state that

> those who are the most deeply devoted to a democratic society must be precisely the ones who insist upon excellence . . . the idea for which this nation stands will not survive if the highest goal free men can set themselves is an amiable mediocrity. (p. 160)

Some of those who can stand to heed Gardner's advice are the rabid critics of gifted child education who promote equity for all—all, that is, except gifted kids.

KEEPING TRACK: DESIGNING SCHOOLS AROUND A SOCIOLOGICAL AGENDA

The American public school system is one of the few in the world that educates *every* child, from the most disabled to the most competent. This was not always the case in the 19th century, when children with disabilities were simply kept at home or, in the early 20th century, where they were shuttered away in institutions that offered little more than a place to live out one's life. However, as we have moved forward in our collective thinking and compassion, we have come to appreciate that every child deserves to be educated to the fullest extent of his or her abilities. How to do this is the problem.

For the sake of convenience and common sense, the practice of "tracking" came into being when masses of immigrants began to enter our schools in the early 20th century. Depending on one's abilities and academic accomplishments, students were directed to a track that was either academic or vocational in focus. Although I'm sure cries of

> In low-performing schools, teachers assume that all students are low performing. Teachers do not even consider the possibility that there are students who are gifted and talented. Gifted and talented students are overlooked and not identified because their performance may be at or one year above grade level. Programming and support for these students is often nonexistent as school curriculum and instruction is based upon the belief that all students are low performing. Teachers need to receive professional development on identifying culturally diverse gifted students, but more importantly, how to provide a challenging learning environment and curriculum for them.
>
> *Donna Y. Ford, Harvie Branscomb Distinguished Professor, Vanderbilt University, Nashville, TN*

elitism surfaced even in those early days of tracking, it just made sense to place students in classes that the adults around them thought to be the most beneficial. One track was not superior to the other, as John Gardner (1961) wrote that "the society which scorns excellence in plumbing as a humble activity and tolerates shoddiness in philosophy because it is an exalted activity will have neither good plumbing nor good philosophy: neither its pipes nor its theories will hold water" (p. 86).

But then, the critics of tracking began to emerge, as this practice came to be seen by some as the evil invention of the cultural elite who wanted to maintain two systems of schooling: one for the "smart" kids and another one for everyone else. One of the staunchest critics of tracking is Jeannie Oakes, whose 1985 book, *Keeping Track: How Schools Structure Inequality*, became the Holy Grail to which naysayers of tracking clung to for solace. Stating then (and in her book's second edition, in 2005) that the only people who benefit from tracking are the children of the "Volvo Vigilantes," a not-so-subtle dig at affluent parents who knew how to game the school system to their advantage, Oakes pilloried anyone who dares to say that gifted children need to be taught in a classroom with other smart kids, by teachers who know how to teach beyond rote drill and memorization techniques.

Further, she stated again and again that the lower-track classes are overrepresented with poor and minority children who deserve better; are taught by teachers with less experience and fewer teaching skills, therefore repressing student engagement in the learning process; and are filled with disruptive troublemakers who detract from the learning of students who actually want to succeed.

And you know what? On these latter three points, Oakes is correct. But her solution is not to analyze what can be done to enhance the learning environment for students in the lower track classes; rather, she wants to eliminate the very places where students *are* successful and place all students in a heterogeneous environment where no one is actually learning at the level that legitimately challenges his or her personal level of competency. I believe my mother would say this is "throwing out the baby with the bathwater."

Oakes is not alone in her indictment of gifted and highly capable students—or their parents. Perennial thorn-in-the-side author Alfie Kohn, in a ripping 1998 article titled "Only For *My* Kid: How Privileged Parents Undermine School Reform," stated that "there is no national organization called *Rich Parents Against School Reform*, in part because there doesn't need to be" (p. 569). He went on to explain (accuse?) that tracked courses are seldom designed for legitimate, pedagogical purposes. Instead, citing an earlier study (Wells & Serna, 1996) of detracking in racially mixed schools, Kohn described them as "a naked grab for artificially scarce benefits by those with the power to get them" (p. 271). Kohn seems to believe that every parent of a gifted kid in America is part of a grand conspiracy to downgrade education for every kid who isn't theirs. Sadly, some of Kohn's good points about how to improve instruction for all students get lost in his biased rhetoric that serves little purpose other than to inflame his readers. (I see Alfie Kohn as the Donald Trump of education—a smart man with so much hubris that it's hard to take him seriously.)

Another researcher, Anne Wheelock (1995), an avid supporter of detracking, stated in an article titled "Winning Over Gifted Parents" that in her *extensive* analysis of one school district in Washington state, gifted parents will be convinced that heterogeneous grouping is beneficial when given evidence that "inclusive schooling offers all students the type of education usually reserved for gifted students" (p. 17).

I'm not sure why a common sense solution to teaching children—placing them in classes with kids similar to them in measured ability and/or achievement—became a cultural war on parents of gifted kids, but that's the cesspool in which the debate over tracking now resides. Also, almost every school in America *does not* have the rigid, tracked system of the early- to mid-20th century, where a child was pegged at an early age for inclusion in one level of class from which no deviation was allowed. In today's schools, in fact, the term itself—*tracking*—is an anachronism, replaced with a more subtle and realistic concept: *ability grouping*. With ability grouping, a particular student with a penchant for math might be in the high-level geometry class while being in a less rigorous language arts or history class. In fact, the National Association for Gifted Children adopted an official position in 1991 explicitly endorsing ability grouping while dismissing tracking as ineffectual. Specifically, the statement reads (in part):

> to abandon the proven instructional strategy of grouping students for instruction at a time of educational crisis in the United States will further damage our already poor competitive position within the rest of the world, and will renege on our promise to provide an appropriate education for all children. (p. 1)

I'm not sure I'd have brought in the international comparison piece, as it still implies winners and losers, but the "reneg[ing] on our promise . . ." line makes perfect sense to me.

And, if NAGC support isn't good enough for you, then perhaps the results of a 1995 study by Brewer, Rees, and Argys will convince you of the negative impact of heterogeneous grouping on gifted kids. After studying 3,900 10th graders in all types of math classes—heterogeneously and homogeneously grouped—the authors found this:

> the conventional wisdom on which tracking policy
> is often based—that students in low-track classes . . .
> are hurt by tracking while others are unaffected—is
> simply not supported by very strong evidence . . .
> several other recent analyses have come to similar
> conclusions. There is clearly a case for detracking
> on equity grounds, however, as a result, students in
> upper track classes may suffer major losses in achieve-
> ment test scores. (p. 212)

More recently, researchers (Collins & Gan, 2013) examined the Dallas, TX, public schools in which students were grouped by ability in their classes. The results showed that math and reading scores rose for *both* high-performing and low-performing students in classes that were homogeneously grouped by previous school performance—a result that would surprise few in-the-trenches educators.

Another recent study went a long way to disprove the myth that nongifted students, or those who were "marginal" candidates for gifted program inclusion, perform better academically when placed alongside identified gifted students in classrooms. In this 2013 study of 14,000 fifth graders, the researchers (Bui, Craig, & Imberman, in press) analyzed students' standardized test scores in math, science, social studies, and language arts, comparing those "marginal" candidates to those who did not qualify at all for gifted program inclusion. Even though the marginal students had been placed in a gifted program, their test scores were no better than students not involved in the gifted classes. Contradicting the popular belief that lower ability students "rise to the occasion" when surrounded by higher achieving classmates, no such increases were noted. And one has to wonder whether the teachers in the gifted program had to adjust downward their curriculum rigor to accommodate those students who didn't qualify for placement in it.

As emphasized earlier, placing nongifted students in classrooms with those who are gifted is a "feel good" strategy meant to prop up the lower achievers—a sociological response to an educational issue. The Dallas-based study cited above is one more indicator of the error of trying to artificially equalize unequals. As Stephanie Tolan, an advocate for highly and profoundly gifted students, has stated, "you don't have the moral right to hold one child back to make another child feel better" (Meckstroth & Kearney, 2013, p. 289).

Happily, the trend toward detracking has lost some of its steam in the past decade, as evidenced by an analysis from the Brookings Institute (Loveless, 2013) which showed that ability grouping in fourth and eighth grades has increased steadily since 2000 in both math and reading, a trend that surprised the researchers due to "the vehement opposition of powerful organizations" (p. 13) to the practice. Today, about three-quarters of all American elementary and middle school students are in some type of ability-grouped classes. Even teachers are increasingly comfortable with this trend, as the Brookings data showed that 71% of fourth-grade teachers in 2009 agreed with ability groping in reading—a rise from 28% a decade earlier. A similar (but less dramatic) upward trend was found in eighth-grade teachers, too. Yet the idea that all kids will learn in the same inclusive environment is still rampant in some elementary schools—the years where distinct gifted programs are most likely to be offered (and eliminated.) Recognizing this reality, Jeannie Oakes (2005), now the Director of the Ford Foundation's Educational Opportunity and Scholarship Programs, stated in the preface to *Keeping Track*'s second edition that "the most sobering lesson is that, despite the solid evidence and considerable reform of the past 20 years, most American schools are still keeping track" (p. xii).

To which I'd add . . . amen to that! For when sociology trumps common sense regarding educational placement and practice, the wrong experts—like Jeannie Oakes and Alfie Kohn—are being listened to. I'd rather be on the side of the 71% of teachers who are on the frontline of classroom instruction than supporting the rhetoric of folks like Oakes and Kohn who pontificate from afar.

HEY! EVERYONE COULD BE GIFTED, RIGHT?

Everything has its limit—iron ore cannot be educated into gold. —Mark Twain

Much of the criticism on tracking comes from individuals who believe that we are underestimating the intelligence of many children, especially those from poverty, or who speak little English, or who are members of a minority group (excepting Asians, who are generally overrepresented in gifted programs). I'm not here to refute this assumption; in fact, too often children *in general*, including gifted kids, are given short shrift when it comes to adults recognizing and embracing their capabilities. So, if a kid smells bad or dresses shabbily, or has terrible handwriting, a bad attitude, or an attention span of a nanosecond, educators and others often question how such a person could be intelligent. It takes an observant, thoughtful adult to see beyond the disguises that often mask giftedness and capture the intellectual essence that *is* this child. As Thomas Jefferson wrote, "Let us in education dream of an aristocracy of achievement arising out of the democracy of opportunity." Such opportunity does not begin with a specific program or classroom structure; it starts with an attitude that allows one to get beneath the surface of one's academic veneer.

However, having this insightful, respectful attitude toward finding giftedness in kids who don't "look smart" or "act smart" is a far cry from what is now hitting the popular media with a vengeance: anyone can become gifted as long as you try hard enough. Naming this phenomenon "Coercive Egalitarianism 2.0 (CE 2.0)," Dr. Stephen Schroeder-Davis (2012) explained that CE 2.0 is a branch of popular literature that asserts that "aptitude is not a factor in talent development, but rather, the distinguishing factor that separates skill levels is the amount of practice undertaken by individuals" (p. 6).

The book that epitomizes this "I can work myself into giftedness" attitude is Malcolm Gladwell's *Outliers: The Story of Success*. Published in 2008, *Outliers* posits that what separates the intellectual chaff from the wheat is not aptitude, but practice. Naming it the "10,000-hour rule," Gladwell used as the basis for his argument the work of psychologist K.

Anders Ericsson, whose 1993 article, "The Role of Deliberate Practice in the Acquisition of Expert Performance" raised this issue initially. In that article, Ericsson and colleagues (1993) examined the performance of violinists at Berlin's elite Academy of Music. What Ericsson found was that the distinguishing factor separating the academy's most and least accomplished musicians was not the quality of their initial skill level but rather, the amount of time spent in intense, focused "deliberate practice." Over many years, those violinists who practiced for 10,000 hours became the best of the best, no matter what skill level they had when they entered the academy. The also-rans were those who practiced less. Gladwell went on to cite another set of musicians, The Beatles, and claimed that their arduous, early career performance schedule (1960–1962) in Hamburg, Germany, amounted to the 10,000 hours of practice they needed to become world-class musicians. As Gladwell wrote in his book, "The Beatles would not have become The Beatles without Hamburg" (p. 50).

Schroeder-Davis (2012) took serious exception to Gladwell's conclusion about The Beatles by stating this:

> Gladwell omitted references to dozens of bands that were doing the same thing at the same time and did not revolutionize popular music. Ever hear of Rory and the Hurricanes? They were the headliners in Hamburg *for whom The Beatles opened.* Let me be clear: The Beatles' experience in Hamburg was, in fact, integral to their development, perhaps even a 'game changer,' but those hours of practice would not have resulted in The Beatles' legacy had they not been profoundly gifted as well, a factor to which Gladwell gives but a passing nod. (p. 6)

Schroeder-Davis also pointed out a flaw in Gladwell's logic when he uses the Berlin violinists as the basis for his assertion: These students were *already* world-class performers—you couldn't get into the Academy of Music if you *weren't* world-class! Unwilling to "sacrifice giftedness on the altar of effort," Schroeder-Davis knew what should be obvious: Innate abilities play at least some role in life success.

By the dozens of books and hundreds of articles that have extolled the benefits of the 10,000-hour rule in sports, business, nursing, etc. (including an interesting piece in Britain's *The Guardian* titled "Guitar Zero: Can Science Turn a Psychologist Into Jimi Hendrix?"), it's obvious that this readily graspable concept designed to make everyone feel good about their own potential has mass appeal. But as David Bradley pointed out in his 2012 article "Why Gladwell's 10,000-Hour Rule Is Wrong," 10,000 hours is not a magic number. In one study in which college students were trained to memorize long strings of digits, they became "expert" after only 500 (boring) hours of practice. And when Gladwell cited Bill Gates as another example of deliberate practice being the reason for his success, he forgot to cite that not all of Gates' practice was deliberate—some was incidental, such as having early access to a computer at age 13, at a time when computers were rare. Further, to reach the 10,000-hour pinnacle, one would need to practice 90 minutes *every day* for 20 years or 3 hours *every day* for 10 years. So if anyone suggests using this 10,000-hour rule as a way to encourage young children to be successful . . . you best have a lot of patience. As Bradley concluded:

> we do not know yet whether anyone with strong enough motivation and the spare time could become a virtuoso simply through deliberative practice, year in year out. So, while practice may get some of us close to perfection, for many of us, it is an unattainable goal. (p. 2)

MORE ON THE UNIVERSAL GENIUS

Gladwell's book prompted many clones, including David Shenk's 2010 volume, *The Genius in All of Us: Why Everything You've Been Told About Genetics, Talent, and IQ Is Wrong.* The title of this book alone should warn you that the author is going to take some overarching swipes at the nature/nurture argument about the basis of intelligence that was proposed by Francis Galton in 1874. And swipe he does.

Relying on the new science of epigenetics (really?), which is the study of how environmental stimuli, hormones, and nerve impulses alter our genes, Shenk proposed one of his many platitudes: that our world does not have a "talent scarcity" but rather, a "latent talent abundance." So how does an individual take advantage of this latent talent and turn it into genius? Simple! The 10,000-hour rule! If practice, practice, practice is the only way to get to Carnegie Hall, then it is also the way to release the genius hidden deep in your psyche. Relying on anecdote after anecdote of famous individuals (almost all men, by the way), Shenk revealed Mozart as someone whose practice, not inherent musical majesty, led him to eminence at an early age. And because Ted Williams would practice his swing for so long that his fingers bled, that goes to prove that sticking with something you love and persevering through the pains and failures will allow you to become a Red Sox player with a few seasons of a .400 batting average.

Warning us that we can't allow ourselves to think anymore using our old paradigms of intelligence, Shenk included a chapter in his book titled, "How to Be a Genius," which led critic Suki Wesling (2010) to state that this book is a great "self-help manual to those who feel like failures" (para. 1). Like Rory and the Hurricanes, perhaps?

There is an aspirational attraction to a theory that says you can be greater than you think you are, and no one has the right to downplay the efforts of someone who genuinely wants to improve. However, this is a far cry from dismissing the role of heredity (or downplaying it substantially) in determining intelligence. You can't just toss out 150 years of evidence to the contrary by giving a snappy subtitle to your book, as Shenk has done.

The implication made by Shenk and others who believe that giftedness is universal, emerging in some while remaining latent in others, puts gifted child advocates in a tough spot. For if we deny that gifted children exist or, as Shenk (2012) wrote in his book, "no one is genetically designed for greatness" (p. 43), then what real purposes do gifted classes serve? I can already hear school administrators trying to save a few bucks by telling their faculty that the gifted program will be eliminated and the monies formerly spent on the program will be channeled to *all* classrooms to help the latent geniuses bloom.

Shenk's book was well-received by many prominent publications—*The New York Times*, *The Guardian*, The Freakonomics Blog—but it is Wesling's (2010) final analysis that really hits home:

> It's inspirational to say that we can change a child's life by believing he has the potential to excel, but to deny the needs of (gifted children) on a theory that inspires us will not lead us any closer to the goal of having a functional society of well-educated adults. Shenk's blueprint is interesting, but it's not a blueprint for gifted—or any—education. (para. 19)

Two other related books that deflate the genetics of superior performance to nonentity status are Matthew Syed's (2010) *Bounce: Mozart, Federer, Picasso, Beckham, and the Science of Success* and Daniel Coyle's (2009) *The Talent Code: Greatness Isn't Born. It's Grown. Here's How*. Condensed below is a taste of the snake oil each is trying to sell.

Syed, a sports writer for the *Times of London* and a former two-time Olympian in table tennis, climbs into bed, metaphorically speaking, with Malcolm Gladwell. In fact, he cited *Outliers* three times in the first 17 pages of his book. Adhering to the 10,000-hour rule like a burr clings to Velcro, Syed (2010) claimed through one story after another that genetics plays no role in extraordinary performance. Focusing mostly on athletes—Roger Federer, David Beckham, Tiger Woods—Syed claimed that it is only through the practice-failure-practice doctrine that one becomes exceptional. He titled this first section of his book, "The Talent Myth," and used himself as his own case study—someone who was born into humble surroundings and still rose to the top: "no silver spoon. No advantages. No nepotism. Mine was a triumph of individuality" (p. 4). He then told his personal story of a teacher/coach who turned his entire British neighborhood into a hotbed of exceptional table tennis players, with himself being Exhibit A. Due to this personal experience with the 10,000-hour rule, Syed claimed that talent is a "defunct concept," insisting that each individual has the potential to tread the path of excellence. But as

Michael Henderson (2010), a former colleague of Syed's at *The Times* wrote, Syed is "eager to find profundity where none exists" (para. 9).

The danger in a book like *Bounce* is that it is the equivalent of a fast food diet: enjoyable, but not sustaining. Still, this didn't keep Syed from being named "Best New Writer" by the British Sports Book Association in 2011, and from his book becoming a best seller in Britain and America. I am not advocating that you read this book—if you've read *Outliers,* or even my review of its contents on the previous few pages, then you get the gist of *Bounce*, too—but it is important to be alert to the absurdities that are gussied up through the beauty of compelling biographies and vivid storytelling. *Bounce* does this well, but its premise is flawed. As astronomer Carl Sagan said, "Absence of evidence is not evidence of absence."

In *The Talent Code*, Daniel Coyle (2009) used *scientific* evidence to prove that science doesn't have much of a role in the development of talent. If that sounds like doublespeak, welcome to Coyle's world. He started his book, as most pop psychologists do, with a compelling story, this one about 13-year-old Clarissa. Poor Clarissa is a disheveled, uninteresting waif with no particular aptitude for anything. Then, during a 6-minute block of her music lesson one day (conveniently captured on video), she performs like a virtuoso while performing Woody Herman's *Golden Wedding* on her clarinet. This intrigued Coyle to such a degree that he wrote:

> This is not a picture of talent created by genes; it's something far more interesting. It is 6 minutes of an average person entering a magically productive zone . . . they have entered a zone of accelerated learning that, while it can't quite be bottled, can be accessed by those who know how. In short, they've cracked the talent code. (pp. 5–6)

After reading this, I half expected Rod Serling to enter the picture with a whirling backdrop of eyeballs, wooden doors, and breaking glass. Instead, what I got treated to was Coyle's "revolutionary scientific discovery" of how a neural insulator called myelin is the motherlode of personal excellence. Myelin's been around for a long time in human brains and, Coyle (2009) stated in his book, it gets thicker and thicker when we practice particular activities. And this thick myelin is good, for the thicker it gets, the more speed and skill you develop—hence, the 6-minute "Clarissa Zone," so named by Coyle. (I am *not* making this up!) Sadly, however, myelin is "imperceptible—we can't see or feel it and we can sense its increase only by its magic-seeming effects" (p. 6).

So there you have it: A theory of talent development that is based on a substance that can't be measured, downplaying the role of genetics while using a physiological reaction to bolster a claim. Huh? Stating that the secret to unlocking the talent code is to perform *deep practice* (there's the 10,000-hour rule again), *ignition* (the "primal cues" that motivate you to achieve), and *master coaching* (teachers who encourage deep practice and ignition), you are destined to become as exceptional as Jessica Simpson—pop singer extraordinaire and an exemplar used by Coyle to back up his claims. Seriously?

One reviewer (Aesopian, 2012) summed up Coyle's assertions thusly: "Get someone passionate about something and make them practice for years under an experienced coach and they'll get good (unless they don't)" (para. 16).

Not to be outdone, Malcolm Gladwell decided to write yet another tome on the unimportance of high intellect and strong ambition. In *David and Goliath: Underdogs, Misfits, and the Art of Battling Giants* (2013), Gladwell used selected case studies of miscreants who made it big. In this book, Gladwell is still gnawing on his *Outliers* misguided premise: innate abilities matter little in long-term success. What *really* matters are overcoming personal hurdles and family troubles—and of course, his selected biographies of such winners all prove his point. Yeah, right . . . Gladwell also used one case study to prove that in order to succeed, you must keep your ambitions in check. He pointed to Caroline Sacks (a pseudonym) who loved science and decided to go to Brown University instead of the less prestigious University of Maryland. Alas, that decision (according to Gladwell) was the start of her academic demise, for after a bit of time at Brown, poor Caroline began to feel she wasn't very smart after all, so she changed her major to liberal arts. Tragic, right? Well, Gladwell would have you think so, for he contended that if she had attended the University of Maryland instead, her self-confidence would have been maintained and she'd now be a scientist. I'm not sure of the moral here, but it seems to be something like "Second rate is good enough." Using his logic, I guess the path to success for the underdogs of the world is to lower their ambitions to an easily attainable level.

BACK TO RORY AND THE HURRICANES

It might seem to be a stretch to couple the detracking crowd (Oakes, Kohn) with the "everyone is a latent genius" authors whose books are mentioned above. However, the two phenomena share a close resemblance: both are based on the idea that the best way to deal with giftedness is to make believe it doesn't exist at all in children—rather, it is "created" through effort, practice, and the occasional raw deal that life hands you.

Those who choose to deny any biological basis for giftedness seem very selective in which branches of genetics they prune. I can't imagine that any of these authors would deny that hair color, height, predisposition to diseases or nearsightedness, or a tendency toward obesity have at least some basis in the genes we are dealt. If this is so for virtually every other element of our existence since birth, then how can they deny the rightful place of genetics in determining one's innate level of intellect?

No one will refute the potential impact of your personal lifestyle or of the environment in which you exist on the quality of your daily life. So even if you were born with a predisposition toward heart disease, exercise and a healthy diet can mitigate against your chances of coronary impairment. And although there's not much you can do about increasing your height, even some great basketball players who didn't "measure up" in the typical sense succeeded professionally. Case in point: Tyrone "Muggsy" Bogues who, at 5' 3" was the shortest man ever to play in the NBA, becoming a point guard for the Charlotte Hornets and having a successful 10-year career with them. So *of course* a person's environment and personal lifestyle choices affect the quality of their years on Earth ... but so do genetics. By dismissing or discounting the relevance of genetic material on particular aspects of one's being—

like intelligence—some very smart people are making some very dumb assertions and, sadly, carrying a large number of Americans along with them.

Rory and the Hurricanes did not have in abundance what The Beatles possessed naturally: an innate talent in music that was enhanced by their practice, not determined by it. Gifted children are the same: They exist from birth. As wise parents and other educators of these children know, we ignore the early signs of giftedness at our peril. Treating all children the same for the sake of equity is, in fact, the most unfair thing we can do to *every* child.

One additional aspect of the Gladwell et al. crowd is their devotion to giftedness (a term they eschew) as being synonymous with eminence. The examples cited are noted musicians, professional athletes, and Nobel laureates, yet those who live and work with gifted children know that giftedness is more than the sum of their achievements. In fact, some highly gifted people fail to achieve in any visible ways. So the question becomes this: Is giftedness *something you do*, or is it *someone you are*? Let's explore that question in the next chapter.

CHAPTER 4

IS GIFTEDNESS SOMETHING YOU DO OR SOMEONE YOU ARE?

y first year of teaching in a gifted program was in a small town in rural, northeastern Connecticut. It was a "pull-out" program that met three half-days each week for fourth through sixth graders who had been identified as gifted. This was the first time that Stafford Springs was going to have a G/T program and, because there was no set curriculum that I was given to teach, I was allowed to do whatever I chose with my 30+ students. Being new to all of this "gifted stuff"—my previous teaching experience had been with children with learning disabilities—I opted to split my time between designing lessons about creativity and critical thinking with additional opportunities for the students to conduct independent studies on any topic of their personal interest.

The majority of the kids grasped fully this golden ticket of educational autonomy, pursuing projects as diverse as Civil War photography, whale ecology, and writing the Great American Novel. And although the projects varied in quality, our classroom was usually

> In order for gifted kids to have a satisfying and appropriately challenging school experience, they should feel they are partners in their own education. They're empowered when the adults in their world take time to guide them through the steps to self-advocacy: exploring and reflecting on their strengths, interests, and learning styles; discovering options and opportunities that fit their needs; and then becoming proficient at successfully communicating what they want. Adding self-advocacy to their "skill portfolio" will help our brightest kids navigate their own wonderfully unique paths to graduation . . . and beyond.
>
> *Deb Douglas, Former gifted coordinator and past president, Wisconsin Association for the Talented and Gifted, Madison, WI*

abuzz with vibrant young minds pursuing what they so wanted to explore: the worlds outside or inside of themselves.

Except Greg. A quiet, quirky boy who often entered the classroom late ("I forgot it was Wednesday!"), much of Greg's time was spent exploring the possibility of what he might want to study in depth. One week it related to math, the next to science, and week after week the same thing happened: not much of anything. It wasn't that Greg wasn't interested in doing any work, and our frequent conversations were all the evidence I needed to prove that Greg was a very intelligent 11-year old. It was just that he couldn't decide on that one special something that he wanted to pursue.

When I was observed by our school's principal, one of his first comments to me was about "Wandering Greg." I explained that Greg hadn't yet found his particular niche of passion, but that his interests were broad and deep; I suspected that he would eventually settle into something big to study. My principal explained that this gifted program was under tremendous scrutiny by both local educators and the community in general and that I had best figure out a way to get Greg on the path to success. If not, Greg would be axed from the gifted program for his lack of progress. In essence, Greg was expected to *prove* his giftedness through his classroom actions. Having big ideas alone was not going to be enough.

This quandary that I confronted during my first year of teaching gifted kids is one that still exists today in our field: Do you have to *prove* you are gifted by completing projects and getting good grades, or is your high intellect and deep insight enough to qualify you as a gifted person?

Let's start with the latest salvo into this conundrum that continues to divide the gifted education field into two very distinct camps: the *something you do* advocates for gifted children and the *someone you are* adherents. It comes to us courtesy of the National Association for Gifted Children, which, in 2010, officially adopted a new definition of giftedness. It reads as follows:

> Gifted individuals are those who demonstrate outstanding levels of aptitude (defined as exceptional ability to reason and learn) or competence (documented performance or achievement in top 10% or rarer) in one or more domains. Domains include any structured activity with its own symbol system (e.g. mathematics, music, language) and/or set of sensorimotor skills (e.g. painting, dance, sports). (para. 5–6)

Count 'em: That's four parenthetical expressions in one paragraph, which led me to believe that this definition was written by a committee that couldn't quite agree on anything (and yes, a task force of 15 people did draft this definition). But that's just the first paragraph of three, making a total of 224 words needed to define giftedness. And should you need further explanation, the rationale for this definition is provided in an accompanying position statement, also courtesy of NAGC.

Convolution has never been my friend, so this new definition sent my head spinning. First, it focuses almost entirely on performance, with just a passing nod given to inherent aptitude. Second, it virtually ignores any aspect of giftedness that does not relate to academic or other domain-specific fields, yet as any parent of a gifted child can tell you, emotional intensity is often part of the gifted child package. Third, by focusing so heavily on giftedness being a visible action, it ignores kids like Greg whose high abilities have not yet manifested themselves into anything concrete.

This definition set up a maelstrom of complaints and concerns within the gifted education community, including a broad-based critique by me (Delisle, 2012), in which I wrote that I found

> this approach to giftedness both utilitarian and self-ish . . . Our field's uniqueness lies not in the curriculum we offer our students nor the educational methods we use to develop their talents; rather, our field's focus since it began a century ago has been to recognize the unique cognitive and affective facets of a gifted child's life and then finesse school experiences to enhance these traits. (p. 1)

Supporters of NAGC's utilitarian view of giftedness, as well as those who had a hand in its creation, defended it strongly once the criticism began. Paula Olszewski-Kubilius, President of NAGC when this maelstrom started, stated in one of her regular communications with NAGC members in 2011 that gifted education needed to "consider making talent development, rather than giftedness, the major unifying concept of our field and, most importantly, the basis of our practice" (p. 2). And Kristie Speirs Neumeister (2012), one of the Task Force members responsible for this new definition, argued that "this definition embraces different theoretical perspectives, yet is practical enough to be operationalized by educators and policy makers advocating on behalf of gifted students" (para. 3). She doesn't go on to explain what this operationalization might look like; indeed, it seems a premature call to state its practical utility when, at the time, not even one state had adopted this definition.

One of the reasons that those folks who dislike this definition register their concern is that its writing and adoption seem to have caught many people by surprise. It appeared on the NAGC website in 2010, just after the organization's Board of Directors voted to approve it. Yet a draft version of this definition was never vetted to the membership, leaving many to ask, "Where did this come from?" The lack of transparency seemed obvious to me, but in response to my criticism of the secretive nature of this definition's birth, Speirs Neumeister (2012) wrote that "as the Board of Directors is elected to represent the membership, this process did ensure transparency as well as validation of the ideas reflected in this new definition" (para. 5). She further went on to state that she hopes "these discussions could be held with respect to the individuals who have dedicated their time and intellectual energy to contribute to our field" (para. 6), implying that the criticism of the product and the process have been anything but polite. Just one question: How *respectful* is it to impose this definition before airing it publically to the very people who advocate most strongly for gifted kids—the nearly 7,000 members of NAGC?

To those individuals who do not live and breathe gifted education on a daily basis, this whole brouhaha might seem like little more than an academic sparring match. But it is *much more* than that: If endorsed by states and local school districts, this new definition transforms our entire field into one where the primary focus is not children, but curriculum. Which seems to be just fine with those who do not call themselves "gifted child educators" but instead "talent developers."

Speaking of talent developers, three of them proposed *yet another* conception of giftedness that reads like a steroid-fueled version of the NAGC definition. Stating that their definition is "comprehensive and useful across all domains of endeavor" (Subotnik, Olszewski-Kubilius, & Worrell, 2011), the definition reads as follows:

> Giftedness is the manifesting of performance that is clearly at the upper end of the distribution in a specific talent domain even relative to other high-functioning individuals in that domain. Further, giftedness can be viewed as developmental in that in the beginning stages, potential is a key variable; in later stages, achievement is the measure of giftedness; and in fully developed talents, eminence is the basis on which this label is granted. Both cognitive and psychosocial variables play an essential role in the man-

ifestation of giftedness at every developmental stage, are malleable, and need to be deliberately cultivated. (p. 176)

Although this definition does pay homage to the cognitive *and* affective development of gifted children, it's bottom line is this: No matter what advanced abilities you show in childhood, you will not be considered a gifted adult unless you reach eminence. Thus, an adult with a high IQ, a propensity for deep thought, and a range of emotions that is stunningly different from others around him loses a bit of the giftedness each year that eminence isn't reached.

Even researchers who are in general agreement with this view of giftedness question whether "eminence" is its endpoint. McBee, McCoach, Peters, and Matthews (2012) reacted to the impracticality of this definition by writing:

> Whether a given child may or may not have the potential to achieve eminence in some domain is almost completely irrelevant to a given day in the life of the student and the classroom teacher. The search for long-term prediction of eminence does not help K–12 schools in the development of advanced academic skills. (p. 212)

Further, these same authors questioned how one defines "eminence." Is it always visible, via a new invention, a book written, a scientific discovery revealed, or can it be "quieter" and not exist in any particular domain at all?

> We suggest that connecting learners with appropriate educational experiences, whose overarching goal is the production of highly trained and ethical individuals who function competently in varied and complex fields of human endeavor, is the proper goal for advanced academics. (McBee et al., 2012, p. 213)

These authors ended their critique by making a statement that is brilliant in its simplicity: "we believe the time has arrived for the [gifted education] field to divide itself into the subdisciplines of high-ability psychology and advanced academics" (McBee et al., 2012, p. 213). This proposed schism may be just the ticket to reengage people into looking at gifted children, first and foremost, as the unique human beings that they are rather than the eminent adults they might someday become. The talent developers? I'm not sure what would distinguish them from *any other* educator—after all, aren't *all* teachers developers of talent?— but if they want to move forward in a different direction, I wish them well in their utilitarian task.

GOING BACK IN TIME

The controversy addressed above had its roots a generation earlier, when one of gifted education's most prominent and prolific advocates, Joseph Renzulli, set the tone for the current debate. In a 1978 article titled "What Makes Giftedness?: Reexamining a Definition," Renzulli argued that the people we notice as gifted and talented in the real world are the ones known for creative productivity—the patents they obtain, the poetry they write, the buildings and theories they construct. To Renzulli, giftedness is less a trait (like IQ) than it is a set of behaviors *based on* traits. He urged his colleagues then—and still does today—to stop talking about gifted *children* and speak instead about children with *gifted behaviors*. Renzulli's conception of giftedness put the emphasis not on a set of testable preconditions (for example, high scores on IQ or achievement tests) but squarely on the shoulders of kids who needed to prove their giftedness through their actions. He even suggested that evidence in human history shows that our most creative producers were not necessarily the smartest people—their abilities were above average, but not necessarily superior. What they *did* possess that made them memorable in the long run were two other traits: task commitment (basically, sustained motivation) and creativity. Combined with their above average intellects, these individuals exhibited *gifted behaviors*.

(Thus, it's doubtful that anyone asked Jonas Salk his IQ once they got their hands on his polio vaccine.) Such a view of giftedness brings to mind a Bible passage—Matthew Chapter 7, Verse 16: "Ye shall know them by their fruits."

Conveniently, Renzulli had published a gifted program template, The Enrichment Triad Model, a year earlier. In this model, all kids receive lessons in creativity and critical thinking, and are exposed to all manner of subjects and individuals that could serve as sparks to ignite their own productivity. And those who did respond by wanting to explore a topic in great depth would be invited into the gifted program to complete said project. Once finished, this child would revolve back out of the gifted program to make room for another potential "child with gifted behaviors."

With a generation of hindsight to guide us, it's easy to see how the talent development approach to giftedness grew out of Renzulli's work. Such views of giftedness, though, do little to assist kids like "Wandering Craig" who, despite high abilities, wouldn't be served in a Renzulli-type program until he got his productive act together. And for those kids who are smart but seldom show it—the gifted underachiever—well, that label no longer applies, as the term itself is oxymoronic.

This on again/off again view of giftedness (sorry...gifted *behaviors*) where the label "gifted" is applied only temporarily, like a henna tattoo that fades in time, makes perfect sense to that long-ago principal of mine (and his contemporaries), who want the gifted program to be a hotbed of productive activity that could be showcased to the public. However, to others, it is not an attractive or sufficient option, as it fails to take into account less visible traits that some, including this boy, possess in abundance:

> I asked my son about what he thought about the idea of giftedness being defined as excelling in a specific domain such as math or soccer. He was quite upset. He found it hard to believe that someone who is sup-posed to know about gifted kids would come up with such a limited view. He said that giftedness to him is how he understands the world, how deeply he views

things, and that isn't measurable by taking a test, getting straight-As, or winning prizes. He said that has always been his problem: teachers want him to get straight-As rather than engage in a dialog about how he interprets literature or an event in history... What now? Will my son be found "not gifted" because his gifts lie in areas outside of specific domains, whatever they are? (W. R., parent of gifted child, personal communication, May 16, 2012)

This continuing debate over what constitutes giftedness—trait based or talent determined?—will likely not go away very soon. As is typical in educational and psychological research, each side will cite evidence of why its view is more valid; each adherent will point out examples of the depth and breadth of their vision, their version, of intellectual might.

Outsiders must look at the gifted education field and wonder if we're legitimate at all, since we can't even seem to agree on the population of kids we are trying to help. I'll offer some suggestions and remedies to change this in this book's later chapters, as the factions that exist today are certainly as deep as the divide between the Tea Party right and the Progressive left. However we define giftedness, through either traits or behaviors or both, the fact remains that countless children are not being served appropriately by the schools and society that are supposed to be putting their welfare above all else. We can do better, for both the kids as individuals and for our nation's intellectual well-being as a whole.

THE GARDNER MACHINE: THE JUGGERNAUT OF "MULTIPLE INTELLIGENCES"

By far the most popular view of intelligence to hit the public eye within the past 30 years is Howard Gardner's 1983 book, *Frames of*

Mind. In that book, Harvard professor Gardner proposed that there is no such thing as overall intelligence—that pesky "g factor" that has been around since the assessment of intelligence began—but that *all* people have a number of intelligences at their disposal—his Theory of Multiple Intelligences (MI). So although some of us have a linguistic flair, others prefer math, while others excel at dance or music or the ability to read people's emotions. Using what he says is a grueling set of criteria to determine the actual existence of a particular intelligence— such as its "evolutionary probability" and "developmental history"— Gardner began with seven distinct intelligences, adding a new one several years later.

When I first read Gardner's work, my initial reaction was, "What's the big deal?" We already knew some people are better at certain things than others, so pinpointing the specific realms of human endeavor didn't seem a particularly original idea. Also, as far back as the 1930s, psychologists like L. L. Thurston identified seven "primary mental abilities," many of which parallel those presented by Gardner. Wasn't this just old news in new packaging?

Yes . . . and the packaging was very good. Flying off the shelves like batteries before a blizzard, *Frames of Mind* became a bestseller. People ate up the fact that it didn't matter if you didn't have a high IQ—you could still be smart! This democratization of the human mind was yet another feel-good notion that did one thing: It equated unequals.

It didn't take long for education publishers to jump on the bandwagon of MI mania and start proposing all kinds of ways to take the MI theory and translate it into classroom practices. Once again, old wine in a new jug. One of the most prolific MI authors, Thomas Armstrong (2009), wrote a book titled *Multiple Intelligences in the Classroom*, which became a bible, of sorts, for classroom teachers who bought into Gardner's ideas. In it, he dissects each of the distinct intelligences and tells teachers what they can do to promote each one through simple classroom activities.

Let's examine just how wrong this is. First, Gardner is a psychologist, not a teacher, and his work was promoted (by him) as a *theory*, which, by definition, can't be applied directly to practice. Second, there is no evidence that if I have a fine voice I will memorize my multiplication facts faster by putting them to verse and singing them out loud. It sounds logical, but is it true? Third, to implement instructional practices willy-nilly, as Armstrong did, because of a book that caught your attention is a prime example of flagrant educational malpractice.

Here's what one of Gardner's most robust critics, Daniel Willingham (2004), had to say about Gardner's work: "What would you think if your child came home from school and repeated that the language arts lesson of the day included using twigs and leaves to spell words?" (p. 19).

Willingham went on to state that most parents would probably wonder about the rationale for this type of hands-on spelling assignment, and the rationale would be this: Such instructional tactics will help you to capitalize on your "naturalistic intelligence," the newest of Gardner's eight intelligences—the one that focuses on those students whose strength is that they are "one with nature."

If you multiply this example by 10,000, you still would not reach the number of absurd practices that have been developed under the guise of following the MI theory. Even the evidence provided in a study by some of Gardner's collaborators (Kornhaber, Fierros, & Veenema, 2004) is mixed, at best, and indecipherable, at worst, on the effects of using MI practices in classrooms. Examining 41 schools over a 3-year period in a project called SUMIT (Schools Using Multiple Intelligences Theory), the researchers claim that in 78% of the schools, children's achievement test scores increased. Sounds great, huh? The problem is, there were no control or comparison groups used in the study, so even if scores did increase, how can this be attributed directly to MI practices? Researchers cannot make that intuitive leap and expect to be taken seriously.

In a scathing critique of the MI idea, Christopher Ferguson (2009) contended that although Gardner's theory sounds nice, "it is more intuitive than empirical. In other words, the eight intelligences are based more on philosophy than data" (p. 39). Also, by assigning each intelligence equal importance, Gardner makes another big misstep, as Ferguson explained:

Many people like to think that any child, with the proper nurturance, can blossom into some kind of academic oak tree, tall and proud. It's just not so. Multiple Intelligences provides a kind of cover to preserve that fable. "OK, little Jimmie may not be a rocket scientist, but he can dance real well. Shouldn't that count equally in school and life?" No. The great dancers of the Pleistocene foxtrotted their way into the stomach of a saber-toothed tiger. (p. 39)

Ferguson (2009) concluded that without a healthy dose of "g"—that old-fashioned, empirically based intelligence—people won't get very far in life. That some people are unintelligent, while neither fair not politically correct, is still reality. So, even though the MI theory was a good one to postulate, Ferguson contended that its idea didn't really pan out. "Hanging on to the theory for nostalgia or political value," Ferguson wrote, "is not science. It's time that we begin to work with the reality that we have, not the one we wish we had. To do otherwise would be just plain stupid" (p. 39).

Unfortunately, too many gifted child advocates didn't get the "stupid" memo on MI: they still contend that it has a place in our gifted lexicon. So even though Gardner did not make a direct connection between MI and gifted education, many gifted child educators did latch onto it as the next great thing. This was unfortunate, not so much in terms of the classroom activities that were now being done under the MI umbrella, but more so that they would take this expanded view of intelligence (and hence, giftedness) and accept it so uncritically. In my own critique of MI, titled "Multiple Intelligences: Convenient, Simple, Wrong" (Delisle, 1996), I stated that "Multiple Intelligences distributes giftedness equally among various talent areas . . . which is a politically correct but intrinsically *incorrect* notion of what intelligence is" (p. 21). And Willingham (2004), after years of study on the MI theory, concluded with this: "all in all, educators would likely do well to turn their time and attention elsewhere" (p. 24). The jury is in— Gardner's MI theory is guilty of wishful thinking.

If only Gardner had titled his tome "The Theory of Multiple Talents," that would have been more indicative of its content. But because it is more provocative to state that you've located new ways to be "intelligent"—well, now, that'll sell a lot more books, won't it?

This wholesale diminishing of high intelligence as some figment of a past generation's imagination is among the most corrosive ideas to permeate education and psychology in quite some time. Try as we might to say that "everyone is gifted in some way," it is simply not true—political correctness be damned! America will only begin to get less dumb when we are ready to acknowledge and celebrate the existence of giftedness as a quality of the few, not the many, and to offer those gifted enough to stand out among their peers with an education worthy of their exceptional minds.

CHAPTER 5

INSTRUCTIONAL PANACEAS THAT AREN'T

S witching gears now, going from the debate about what constitutes giftedness to what we should do with these highly able kids once we find them, let's explore some strategies that were supposed to be *the* answers to how best to serve gifted kids, but have fallen short for multiple reasons, from misinterpretation to oversimplification. There are many of these "innovations" to target, but let's begin with the worst offender, a scourge that has haunted gifted child education since the 1990s.

Every teacher education program should prepare educators to meet the needs of the gifted student. New teachers enter their classrooms armed with ways to accommodate struggling students and manage classroom discipline, but few are ready to address those who are advanced learners. It's not surprising that teachers then fall back to the "give 'em more of the same" or "let them help others" approaches. Changes in preservice teacher education would create educators who pretest to identify mastered material, adapt the curriculum to offer more challenge, provide opportunities for in-depth study, and recommend gifted kids for advanced programs, to name several appropriate practices.

Penny Britton Kolloff, retired teacher educator, Champaign, IL

THE INCLUSIVE CLASSROOM

I was talking with a gifted teenager, Brianna, who was reminiscing about her early days in school. She laughed out loud when she told me that she had had a rough start—she had been kicked out of kindergarten. Seeming to be a pleasant and polite teen, Brianna certainly didn't look to be suspension material. This was her crime: Because the work that her teacher assigned was very easy, Brianna finished it quickly. Instead of waiting around for her classmates to catch up, Brianna went to each of their desks and completed the work for them. "They liked that I did it," recalled Brianna, "and I figured we'd move on to other stuff if we could just get past this easy work." As you might imagine, Brianna's teacher was not keen on this personal intervention, so after several warnings went unheeded, Brianna was suspended until such time that she would be mature enough to simply wait for her classmates to finish their assignments.

Brianna's situation is one faced daily by countless gifted kids who languish in heterogeneous classrooms based on the principles and practices of "full inclusion." Full inclusion blossomed in the early 1990s within the special education community. Until that time, children with severe mental and physical disabilities were often taught in separate classrooms—indeed, in the most severe cases, even separate schools—having little or no daily interaction with children who did not have disabilities. Perhaps the kids with disabilities would share a lunch period or an art class with other students, but their academic subjects were taught to them by special education teachers outside of the regular classroom setting.

The architects of full inclusion—there were many of them— promoted these practices on the grounds of social equity: keeping kids apart from one another due only to their differences in learning is discriminatory. How would kids without disabilities learn to interact with those who have them if they never have a chance to get together? And how will the social skills of children with disabilities improve if they are never together with "regular" kids on whom they could model their own behaviors?

These sociological issues are hard to argue with, unless you want to be perceived as a thoughtless ogre who has no heart. However, in practice, full inclusion fell victim to the same erroneous sequence of implementation that is destined to defeat any new idea: ready . . . fire . . . aim. Teachers who had never had more than an introductory course in special education were now expected to teach kids whose mental capacity was years lower than their ages would indicate. Special education teachers were now to "float" between classrooms where their students were placed, instead of teaching them in a small cluster in a separate classroom. Students without disabilities were expected to be accommodating and accepting of kids who might have random emotional outbursts or who were wheelchair-bound and dressed in a diaper. Even though advocates of full inclusion (Sapon-Shevin, 1994; Stainback & Stainback, 1990) remarked that inclusion is not an *act* but a *process*, involving extensive staff development and changes in school philosophy, curriculum, and teaching methods before it is put in place, the implementation plans went full speed ahead with little attention paid to these prerequisite needs. Critics of this willy-nilly approach to special education spoke out on behalf of those hurt the most by full inclusion: the children themselves. Al Shanker, former President of the American Federation of Teachers, wrote this in 1994: "we need to discard the ideology that inclusion in a regular classroom is the only appropriate placement for a disabled child and get back to the idea of a 'continuum of placements'" (p. 20)

It didn't take long for this noble but misguided idea to permeate the ranks of gifted education programs. One of the most incendiary critics, Mara Sapon-Shevin (1994), contended that gifted education programs were so disruptive to a democratic educational community that they needed to be eliminated (she even refused to allow her daughter to participate in a gifted program, despite her eligibility to enter it). By insinuating that a pull-out gifted program that meets one day a week tells its participants, "you're different, so you have to leave," while sending the classroom teacher a message that "you're incapable of teaching smart children," Sapon-Shevin called for all gifted learners to be taught in regular classroom settings. Then, not only would the "regular" kids get to understand and accept that some kids learn faster, the gifted kids would come to appreciate those who didn't learn as fast as they did. The only thing missing from this wonderful mix of wishful thinking is a two-verse rendition of Kumbaya.

Kathi Kearney (1996), an advocate for all gifted children who focuses most of her work on the highly gifted, realized how harmful full inclusionary practices are for the most capable students: "Instead of working at appropriate academic levels and having an equal opportunity to struggle, [gifted children] spend most of the school day tutoring others in cooperative learning groups or reviewing curriculum that they mastered years ago" (p. 1). Realizing that many school programs for gifted students "are caught between the budget knife and current philosophical movements in education which emphasize heterogeneity" (Kearney, 1993, p. 2), she argued that all schools need to be as accessible *intellectually* as they are accessible to those with physical disabilities. This respect for intellectual diversity in all of its forms—including gifted kids—means that principals would no longer be able to set arbitrary age discrimination standards by denying access to educational options that gifted students are ready and able to pursue; that teachers would no longer be able to assign gifted kids as tutors to classmates, given that the teacher doesn't have the time to get to these students herself; and that students who bully gifted kids as being "nerds" or coerce them into "dumbing themselves down" for social acceptance would be held responsible for their actions. Twenty years later, the same need for gifted kids to receive more comprehensive services than what inclusion can ever offer still exists.

In a 2003 article, I proposed some questions that parents of gifted kids in inclusive settings should ask various stakeholders:

> To the principal: "What provisions are in place within the school district to take advantage of children's gifts or talents? How do you know they are being implemented?"
>
> To the teacher: "What activities and curriculum do you offer that provide both complexity and depth to kids ready to handle both? In what ways are gifted kids interacting with each other in your classroom?"

To the student: "What are you learning that you didn't know before? How are you encouraged to pursue your own interests and passions?" (para. 6–8)

Like other perceived panaceas that came before and subsequent to it, full inclusion did not perform the miracles its advocates intended. Kids still learn at different speeds and in different ways, social acceptance of those who differ from the norm is still spotty, and the realization that there is no one best way to structure school and learning is still accurate.

When the Titanic sank into the North Atlantic, it was on a course its captain thought was correct. It's only because it couldn't change direction fast enough that the Titanic entered oblivion. Such must not be the case for gifted children sailing in a sea of educational indifference sponsored by those who promote a one-size-fits-all approach to learning.

RESPONSE TO INTERVENTION (RTI)

Just as full inclusion was begun by advocates of children with disabilities, such was the birth of RtI. Brought about by the 2004 authorization of the federal Individuals with Disabilities Education Improvement Act (IDEA), RtI was designed as an alternative to the "you're either disabled or you're not" policies that guided many special education programs. In essence, prior to RtI, the only children who would get special education services were those with a diagnosed disability. But with RtI, the focus is on interventions that work to aid the learning of *any* child, not just specialized interventions provided to a few kids identified with a specific learning disability. So even though it was designed with special education in mind, RtI is, essentially, an initiative affecting general education as well.

The National Center for Response to Intervention (n.d.) posted this (convoluted) description of RtI on its website:

RtI includes a combination of high-quality, culturally and linguistically responsive instruction; assessment; and evidence-based intervention. Comprehensive RtI implementation will contribute to more
meaningful identification of learning and behavioral
problems, improve instructional quality, provide all
students with the best opportunities to succeed in
school, and assist with the identification of learning
disabilities and other disabilities. (p. 1)

See why I label RtI as a panacea? It's got something for *everyone*!

You might have noticed, though, that the term *gifted* is absent
within this RtI model. To me, this is a good thing, as we could, as a
field, continue to concentrate on how best to serve gifted students
without the mechanizations of a complex system that was not designed
for them. But no, not willing to leave well enough alone, many in the
gifted community grasped onto RtI as the solution to our field's woes.
If we didn't jump onto this latest bandwagon, we'd be run over by it,
right?

So, two major gifted organizations—NAGC and The Association
for the Gifted, a division of the Council for Exceptional Children
(CEC-TAG)—went full speed ahead in endorsing the RtI principles,
which are these:

1. *Universal screening*: "All students and their educational performance are examined in order to ensure that all have an equal
   opportunity for support" (CEC-TAG, 2009, p. 2).
2. *Progress monitoring*: If gifted kids demonstrate mastery of basic
   content (which is called "Tier 1 Intervention"), they need the
   opportunity to move forward with more advanced learning.
3. *Problem-solving approach*: If kids aren't responding to curriculum, a problem-solving team—educators, counselors, parents—convenes to determine what added interventions (Tiers
   2 and 3) are needed to promote student success.
4. *Fluid and flexible services*: Students get instructional services
   based on their individual needs, not on a specific label that
   identifies them as gifted.

This all sounds great in the abstract, but in everyday practice in schools, RtI is a hugely time-consuming process that, truth be told, does not really have a great impact on gifted kids' learning. Let's be honest: Today's school administrators are obsessed with "bringing up the bottom" when it comes to student achievement. Teachers get this message from their principals, focusing their efforts on those students who are struggling with even Tier 1 (basic) instruction. So if you have a gifted kid who is languishing in boredom with a curriculum 2 years below her level of comprehension, but is performing at an average level in class, it will be the rare teacher who asks, "Hmmmm . . . I wonder why Brianna isn't doing as well as her potential indicates?" And thus, another Brianna bites the dust. She doesn't enter the RtI framework because she simply is seldom on the radar screen of teachers who have other priorities.

Another group of children who often get left aside by RtI are those who are twice-exceptional (2E): gifted kids (exceptionality #1) who also have a disabling condition (exceptionality #2), such as a learning disability or autism. In a frequent, sad twist of fate, many 2E kids don't get diagnosed as . . . anything. Their high intellects are masked by their disabilities, so they don't score highly enough to qualify as gifted, yet their disabilities don't get noticed because they are smart enough to compensate for their deficits so as not to appear disabled. The trick to identifying 2E kids is often a comprehensive assessment by a psychologist (and others), yet through RtI, this is less likely to occur (Gilman et al., 2013). It's not that comprehensive assessment is disallowed under RtI, it just takes a long time to get there. Gilman and her colleagues asserted that the number of gifted child specialists and school psychologists who work to identify 2E children has been diminished by budget cuts, resulting in fewer 2E children getting referred for comprehensive assessments to determine the extent of both their giftedness and their disabilities. The Council for Exceptional Children (2007) recommended that "access to a challenging and accelerated curriculum, while also addressing the unique needs of their disability" (p. 2) is a must for 2E children to thrive in today's schools.

The issues are many when it comes to using RtI to benefit gifted kids:

◇ How will teachers be trained to notice when gifted students are not performing at levels that their abilities indicate?

◇ Will gifted kids who underachieve be noticed as anything other than "lazy"?

◇ Considering that advanced assessment tools are supposed to be used by classroom teachers as a form of performance review of students, what are these instruments and how do teachers gain access to them?

I'm afraid there are more questions than answers when it comes to using RtI with gifted students. The RtI designers freely admit that their work was not aimed at gifted learners, so trying to fit that round peg into a very square hole just seems to be more effort than it's worth.

Can't we just wait a few years until RtI exits and another "solution" enters the picture? I'm good with that.

NO CHILD LEFT BEHIND: IN THE WAKE OF ITS DEMISE

Although NCLB will soon be nothing but a sad reminder of good intentions gone bad, its implementation from 2002–2013 hampered the learning of millions of gifted kids nationwide—and may continue to do so in years ahead.

A little bit of NCLB history: Overwhelmingly approved by a bipartisan Congress in 2001 (who ever thought President George W. Bush and Senator Ted Kennedy would agree on *anything*!), the bill was signed into law in early 2002. (Ironically, NCLB expired in 2007, but because the U.S. Congress didn't authorize a replacement, its provisions stayed in effect.)

The underlying premise of NCLB was that if states developed rigorous, standards-based, measureable academic goals for all students, and teachers used these standards as a basis for their teaching, then overall student performance would improve. According to this legislative mandate, within 10 years of NCLB's implementation, *every child* in America's schools would be proficient in reading and math. Every child.

Individual states were left to design their own assessments, but virtually every student in each state had to complete the *same* assessments. So, the most gifted kid and the most disabled one, the most fluent English speaker and the emerging English language learner (ELL): each had to complete the same paper-and-pencil tests. Also, 95% of every "subgroup" (e.g., special education or ELL) had to be included in the testing regimen, and even the kids in these subgroups had to show a common level of "proficiency" called AYP (Adequate Yearly Progress). If schools did not make AYP from one year to the next, various types of penalties were imposed (under the guise of "school improvement," of course). These penalties could range from needing to write a school improvement plan for schools that weren't proficient from one year to the next, to firing ("restructuring," in government terminology) the school's principal and reassigning the teachers if AYP was not met after multiple years.

There were so many problems with this "one-size-fits-all" approach that it should have been obvious from the beginning that NCLB would be a costly failure: costly in terms of dollars and costly in terms of student and teacher morale.

Here's what began to happen. Because states could develop their own assessments, if they found that not enough students were earning "proficiency" in certain subjects, they simply *lowered the rate needed to pass the tests or designed new assessments that were easier*! (Texas, Colorado, and Missouri were three of the worst offenders in this regard.) Also, teachers and administrators knew that their livelihoods depended on kids making AYP, so students were grilled *ad nauseum* with test preparation classes. It didn't matter if you were a smart kid who could have aced the annual test on the opening day of school, you still had to take test preparation classes or have daily instruction on basic content. Rampant cheating began to occur in some highly publicized cases where teachers, principals, and superintendents began to fudge the numbers and actually change students' test answers before they were scored. And, even schools that made dramatic improvements from one year to the next could be deemed as "failing" if they did not reach the preordained level of proficiency required by state guidelines.

If ever there was a perfect storm of bad logic coupled with bad practice in the world of education, NCLB was it.

The effects of NCLB on gifted children were—and are—as sad as they are disturbing. Because schools were being rewarded for efforts to increase the learning of struggling students, little attention was paid to kids who already excelled. As long as a school met its AYP goal, little else mattered. Thus, services for gifted children began to diminish as gifted students were now being "sprinkled around" elementary classrooms to raise the average performance of every classroom, a practice that defies both logic and research. For instance, as far back as 1992—a decade prior to NCLB—James Kulik, a noted social science researcher, found that highly gifted students that are grouped with intellectual peers gain as much as a year of academic development more than if they are placed in a heterogeneously grouped classroom.

Compounding the problem, individual states began to cut back on gifted services. For example, in 2007, the state of Illinois redirected its $19 million budget for gifted programming into a block grant program, allowing school districts to take what had been funds targeted exclusively for gifted students and apply them elsewhere (Stephens & Riggsbee, 2007). At about the same time, California cut its gifted budget by 18%, and in Connecticut, 22% of school districts slashed or eliminated their gifted programs entirely (Davidson Institute for Talent Development, 2006). The Law of Unintended Consequences was surely at work here: In an effort to cut down on the number of struggling students in schools, the implementation of NCLB created another such class of strugglers—gifted kids. As stated by Stephens and Riggsbee (2007):

> Gifted and talented students struggle because they sit in our classrooms and wait. They wait for rigorous curriculum. They wait for opportunities to be chal-
> lenged. They wait for engaging, relevant instruction that nurtures their potential . . . they become our lost talent. (p. 1)

Why care about how high kids can jump as long as they can clear the lowest bar? These misdirected efforts of NCLB, where test performance was the single criterion by which success was judged, resulted in a watered-down curriculum that focused on a limited range of topics. In a study in Chicago Public Schools that examined the effects of NCLB practices on fifth graders, Neal and Schanzenbach (2007) concluded that because NCLB provided weak incentives to devote extra attention to students who were already proficient, school administrators made an active choice to forego rigor for mediocrity. And in a system of accountability that is built around standardized tests, the amount of time teachers devote to subjects that were not tested—science, social studies, art—dropped dramatically.

The truest gauge of NCLB's success was to be that every student in America would be proficient in math and reading by 2014. (So sad that no one asked what to do with kids whose reading proficiency in *kindergarten* was at a third-grade level . . .) But, as that year approached and it was obvious that this pie-in-the-sky pipedream was not going to come true, panicked school administrators and legislators asked for some leverage. They got it in the form of waivers that have been provided to individual states since 2012 by the U.S. Department of Education. Instead of focusing on NCLB's limited goals, states were invited to draw up a comprehensive reform package that included an emphasis on graduating high school seniors who would be "college and career ready." Also, teacher evaluation was given a more critical look, with at least some part of a teacher's success determined by students' test score increases. States were given the option (and federal dollars) to extend the school day or school year (although few chose this option), and a variety of other innovative ideas were proposed. In essence, states were invited to become "laboratories of school reform" and then, to share their successes nationwide. Thus far, more than 40 states have had their waiver application approved, proving beyond a doubt that the promises made by NCLB promoters were very, very out of whack.

It's too early to judge the success of these waivers on any group of students. But just as NCLB ignored the specific learning needs of gifted kids, so does this new waiver option. Nowhere is it required that gifted children be served or their learning measured appropriately by more rigorous assessment tools and, until such time that that requirement is addressed, it is likely that the children in our schools with the widest discrepancy between what they *are* learning and what they are *capable* of learning will be the gifted kids who lie in wait for something more meaningful and engaging than mere proficiency.

DIFFERENTIATED INSTRUCTION

Every new decade seems to bring about the next-great-wave-of-educational-reform. The Progressive Education movement of the 1930s attempted to turn teachers into social reformers. The Back to Basics movement of the 1950s (and revisited by many states in the 1990s) emerged in response to students' (supposed) inability to master even simple facts. The "open classrooms" of the 1960s–1970s found schools being constructed without interior walls, while its critics contended that a touchy feely, student-centered classroom lacked rigor, discipline, and consistency. Tracking by academic ability . . . a whole language approach to literacy . . . a constructivist approach to teach mathematics organically . . . best-selling books edited by E. D. Hirsch asserting in excruciating detail what every first or second or third grader should know . . . all popular reforms at one time or another.

Ay yi yi! Can we handle any more reforms? Ready or not, here one comes: for 21st-century learners, it's differentiated instruction.

Actually, in theory, differentiated instruction is the strategic bedrock on which the foundation of gifted education rests. Essentially, differentiation takes a look at several factors:

◇ *what* students know already and what they still need to learn (content),

◇ *how* students can demonstrate their knowledge (process),

◇ *what* evidence students provide that documents their learning (product), and

◇ *where* and *under what conditions* students go about learning (environment).

Sure, you can find entire books that focus on differentiation's components in ways far more sophisticated than these—many authors include *depth* and *complexity* as two other necessary ingredients in the differentiation pie—but the basics remain the same: Differentiated instruction endorses the idea that (in this case) gifted students should have access to learning matter that takes into account what they already know so that they might pursue learning avenues that are new, challenging, and engaging.

Sounds perfect, doesn't it? The problem is this: In theory, differentiation is great; in practice, it is harder to implement in a classroom than it is to juggle with one arm tied behind your back. Why? Because those who promote differentiation—and school administrators and education professors are particularly fond of doing so—will argue that if a school has a differentiation mindset, there is no need for specific gifted programs. The logic goes that if *all* teachers are challenging *all* students by offering differentiated lessons to *all* kids, then supplementary, out-of-classroom services for students who excel are redundant. Why "pull out" kids with gifted abilities when you can "pull them in" to a differentiated classroom and reach the same ends? The trouble is, those ends are seldom reached.

Case in point: Holly Hertberg-Davis, a graduate student of Carol Ann Tomlinson, one of the gurus (and a fine one) of the differentiation movement, conducted a 3-year study looking at the impact of differentiated instruction. Teachers were given appropriate training and coaching over an extended period, after which Hertberg-Davis decided to examine whether differentiated instruction had any impact on student learning. As reported by Joanne Jacobs (2010), Hertberg-Davis had this to say: "We couldn't answer the question, because nobody was actually differentiating" (p. 1). In this same article, Jacobs related the experiences of Mike Schmoker, a writer for the publication *EdNext*. In visiting Piney Branch Elementary School in Takoma Park, MD, he found that differentiation was supposed to occur in a classroom of mixed-ability students who were broken into reading groups for part of the day, taught homogeneously for math instruction, and were grouped together without regard to ability for science and social studies. As Schmoker found, "the school . . . offers the 'highly gifted' curriculum for very bright students in the same class with students who are working at grade level. Completely integrating the gifted class didn't work" (J. Jacobs, 2010, p. 1). In a similar article, "When Pedagogic Fads Trump Priorities," Schmoker (2010) stated what would be obvious to any experienced educator: "in every case, differentiated instruction seemed to complicate teachers' work, requiring them to procure and assemble multiple sets of materials . . . and it dumbed down instruction" (p. 22).

Not quite a ringing endorsement for differentiation, eh?

The problem with differentiated instruction is not its design—it's the follow-through. When Professor Virgil Ward coined the term "differential education of the gifted"—DEG—in his 1961 book, *Educating the Gifted: An Axiomatic Approach*, he intended that his principles be applied to gifted students who were in classes with *other* gifted students. More a philosopher than a practitioner, even Ward realized that trying to differentiate instruction in a classroom where students' abilities ran the gamut from below average to superior would be a colossal, and virtually impossible, task. A contemporary of Ward, A. Harry Passow, was equally concerned with differentiation being done right and, in a book chapter in which he explains his generalizations and principles of DEG, Passow (1979) stated explicitly that these ideas be applied to students in *specialized gifted programs*: "Programs for the gifted and talented must be viewed as an integral part of an ongoing educational program of the school system" (p. 451).

Ward, Passow, and many other gifted education experts of the day proposed their views on differentiation at a time when gifted students were often pulled from their "regular" classrooms for a day or more a week to receive specialized instruction with a teacher trained in the principles and practices of gifted child education. Generally, these gifted classes had fewer students, and the range of academic and intellectual abilities was limited, as each child had been identified as gifted. In such an environment, differentiating instruction, while not an easy task, was a manageable one. For the most part, these classes were designed to allow students to pursue some degree of independent work, so differentiation was actually a natural part of the learning agenda. All was well. Differentiated instruction worked in a setting of intellectual and academic homogeneity.

However, in the 1980s, something went awry: Separate gifted programs became less and less popular (more on the reasons why in Chapters 5–7) and regular classroom teachers who, for the most part, had either no or minimal training in gifted education principles, were expected to "pick up the slack" and differentiate instruction for all of their students, including the gifted ones. Gifted education specialists, who heretofore had their own classrooms and their own identified gifted students, were now expected to play a different role: to work inside the regular education classrooms and assist their colleagues with differentiation. Yet another perfect storm was just beyond the horizon: Regular classroom teachers were expected to do more with less, gifted specialists were spread so thinly that their impacts on individual teachers and students were minimal, and gifted students were no longer educated—even one day a week—with other gifted students. Such was the beginning of the demise of purposeful differentiated instruction.

However, on paper, everything sounded rosy! *Every* teacher now became a teacher of gifted students! *Every* teacher was now seeing that student's abilities shine through each school day, not just on that one day a week that the gifted students went to a special program! *Every* student could benefit from the collaborative partnerships between the gifted education specialists and the regular classroom teachers. Even the Association for Supervision and Curriculum Development got into the act (it's always a sign that a new panacea is approaching when *Educational Leadership* promotes it on its cover), publishing at least 675 books, monographs, or articles on differentiation in its influential journal in the past two decades. Seems to me that if it takes 675 publications to explain how differentiated instruction works, something that is supposed to work . . . just doesn't.

Maybe it's human nature to try to take a good idea that works in one setting and try to apply it across the board. That certainly seems to be what happened when Virgil Ward's idea of DEG was morphed into a strategy to be applied in all educational settings. In fact, in a 2008 nationwide study of teachers conducted by the Fordham Institute (Farkas & Duffett, 2008), 84% stated that differentiation was either "somewhat" or "very" difficult. Further, 71% reported that they would like to see the nation rely more on homogeneous grouping of advanced students so that they could move along faster and get into greater depth in their studies. And what happens when gifted students are paired with other students to work on group projects? Seventy-seven percent of teachers say that it is their highest achievers who do the bulk of the work—the others just come along for the ride (and the grade).

So, as much as differentiated instruction sounds like the answer to all of education's woes, we must accept the obvious: It is *not* a strategy that can be called a solution to serving gifted students in American schools, it is *not* a strategy that the majority of educators can accomplish in meaningful ways in heterogeneous classrooms, and it is *not* the same in practice as it is in the theories of Virgil Ward and others who wrote so elegantly on how DEG can benefit gifted students. What differentiation *is*, though, is a cheap way out for school districts to pay lip service to how they meet the needs of gifted children. By spreading the gifted education specialist so thinly among many classrooms, and by eliminating separate gifted classes and programs as a result, the only "success" is fewer dollars spent to educate gifted children. The downward spiral continues . . .

THE COMMON CORE STATE STANDARDS: READY OR NOT, HERE THEY COME

Education in the United States continues to evolve, but it is fairly rare for one idea to be accepted and adopted, simultaneously, by almost every one of the 50 states. However, the Common Core State Standards (CCSS) is one of these noted exceptions.

Beginning in 2009, a national initiative began that was led by state education leaders and legislators to identify what students should know in the areas of English/language arts and mathematics. The sets of standards that were developed were specific enough to give teachers guidance as to what knowledge and skills their students were supposed to master, while providing teachers the latitude to teach in ways that they found inviting and effective. For example, one of the standards in reading is for students to be able to "explain how an author develops the point of view of the narrator or speaker in the text." (A full set of the CCSS is available at http://www.corestandards.org.) Teachers could elect to meet this standard through discussion, role-playing, essay construction, etc. As I wrote in an earlier publication,

> [t]hese Common Core State Standards rely on educators to determine how to best translate these standards into rigorous learning experiences that consider the needs of their students, the expectations of the communities in which they work, and the available resources to support students in their learning. (Delisle & Delisle, 2011, p. 4)

For a nation of educators hungry for something to grasp that had both substance and practicality, the CCSS seemed to be the right fit at the right time. (As of early 2013, more than 40 states had adopted all or part of the CCSS, although some state legislatures are reconsidering the adoption of the CCSS.) Included in the CCSS key design was a K–12 focus that seeks to integrate subject matter, rather than focus on each subject separately. For example, in English/language arts, the domains of reading, writing, speaking, listening, and language are written to mesh with one another rather than to be taught as unique, stand-alone skills. Acquisition of these skills transcends reading alone, as each can be applied to any subject, from biology to European history. This curricular integration is something that gifted child educators have been proposing for decades, so such an approach seems well-suited to the abilities of advanced learners. Further, the CCSS authors (National Governors Association Center for Best Practices & Council of Chief State School Officers [NGA & CCSSO], 2010a) stated that in the area of English/language arts:

> The Standards . . . lay out a vision of what it means to be a literate person in the twenty-first century

. . . [Students who meet the Standards] reflexively demonstrate the cogent reasoning and use of evidence that is essential to both private deliberation and responsible citizenship in a democratic republic. (para. 6)

Even if the CCSS were not designed specifically with gifted students in mind, the above sentiment is a good one for gifted educators to buy into: Students just can't absorb information and spit it back, they have to chew on it a good bit to firmly grasp its meaning and importance.

So far, so good. That's when the critics began to emerge.

Andrew Porter (2011), Dean of the University of Pennsylvania Graduate School of Education, wrote that "the common-core movement is turning into a missed opportunity" (p. 24). His rationale for this conclusion is that the new CCSS, when compared against existing state standards, are not a noticeable improvement:

> To be sure, when we consider state standards in the aggregate, the common-core standards present a somewhat greater emphasis on higher-order thinking. But the key word here is *somewhat*; the difference is small, and some state standards exceed the common core in this respect. (p. 25)

Porter also took issue with the types of assessments used to evaluate students' work in meeting CCSS outcomes, finding them too old school and reminiscent of the test-based assessments that have been around for generations. The hoopla over the CCSS, he found, "may turn out to be much ado about nothing" (p. 25).

Although the underlying rationale for developing a common set of nationwide education standards was to ensure that students are (and this is a key phrase repeated by proponents) "college and career ready" by the end of high school, some critics contend that this can't be done with a "one size fits all" approach to education. Valerie Strauss (2010), an education journalist, wrote in the *Washington Post* that once, schools gave youngsters a chance to learn to read according to their own development. Now, a child who still can't read by the end of the first grade is in deep trouble from which it can be hard to emerge . . . telling teachers that they must teach certain things to each child in a specific grade ignores the notion of individual development. (para. 11)

Although Strauss' concern is directed toward students who have difficulty learning, gifted education advocates make a similar argument. To wit, what happens when a child comes into a particular subject or grade level *already knowing* the core standards? Quoting from the ELA document itself, "the Standards do not define the nature of advanced work for students who meet the Standards prior to the end of senior high school" (NGA & CCSSO, 2010b, para. 18). Thus, although the CCSS might be an improvement over the polyglot of curricular benchmarks that had been endorsed previously by individual states, this is no guarantee that gifted students' learning needs will be addressed any more now than before. And with the continuing need to make certain that struggling students "catch up" to their grade-level peers, classroom teachers may be hard-pressed to provide students who excel with the academic challenges they desire and need. If this scenario sounds all too familiar, it is: What did No Child Left Behind ever do for gifted kids—except leave them *behind*?

Although the English/language arts standards include ways to incorporate literacy into other subject areas (e.g., social studies, science, etc.), that does not seem to be a primary focus. Noting that, Diane Ravitch (2010), an education historian from New York University and former U.S. Assistant Secretary of Education, argued that by focusing so significantly on math and language arts, the other subject areas, by default, are deemed less important. Too, Ravitch is concerned that because each standard has quantifiable measures, anything that is *not* measurable will be given short shrift. Yet, as the old saying goes, "not everything that gets measured is important, and not everything that is important can be measured." Beauty? Truth? Justice? Go ahead—quantify them. Ravitch's message goes beyond the CCSS, though, as she is critical of most of the ways that schools, teachers, and students are judged to be adequate. Believing that "schools…cannot improve if they are judged by flawed messages and continually at risk of closing because they do not meet an artificial goal created and imposed by legislators" (2013, p. xii), Ravitch took swing at any so-called reform that seems intended to help those she perceives as privileged. As she wrote in her 2013 book, *Reign of Error*, "if you want a society organized to promote the survival of the fittest and triumph of the most advantaged, then you will prefer the current course of action" (p. 8). Like many before her, Ravitch pits students against each other in the quest for educational excellence—a losing strategy, indeed, when it comes to addressing the needs of gifted students. More than anything else, Diane Ravitch seems to be a cranky lady with a bullhorn—which means that, sadly, she's loud enough that some will listen to her pronouncements.

Another noted educator whose love affair with CCSS is rather lukewarm is Linda Darling-Hammond, a Stanford University professor who served as President Obama's chief education advisor during his first term's transition. Darling-Hammond pointed to the benefit of local involvement—rather than the centralized focus of a national curriculum—in improving education. Citing the nation of Finland (the current poster child for school improvement), she noted in a 2010 article that standardized tests are few in Finnish schools and curriculum development is done by local teachers, not an overarching body of faraway others. Students are left to define their own weekly learning goals in specific subjects, done in consultation with their teachers. In terms of student assessment, most of it is done in narrative form instead of letter grades, and there are no external standardized tests on which either students or schools are ranked. Every classroom teacher gets 3 years of graduate-level training in education (paid for by the government) prior to becoming a teacher, and each school decides what learning goals fit best with their individual school's students.

Because the high school graduation rate in Finland is 99%; Finnish teens come out #1 in the world on the PISA (Program for International Student Assessment) in the areas of language, math, and science; and more than two-thirds of the country's high school graduates attend universities, it's pretty obvious that something is working well in Finnish schools.

But what *also* comes to mind is how similar the curriculum and assessment pieces that work so well in Finland were once common strategies in the almost-defunct option of "pull-out" gifted programs for gifted students—programs where gifted kids spent a day a week (or more) working alongside other gifted kids. Here is how Darling-Hammond (2010) described a typical Finnish classroom:

> Students are likely to be walking around, rotating through workshops or gathering information, asking questions of their teacher, and working with other students in small groups. They may be completing independent, on-going projects or writing articles for their own magazine. (p. 3)

Hmmm . . . perhaps if we want to examine ways to improve learning in our nation's classrooms, we should look to what gifted child educators did so well in those pull-out programs of yesteryear. Just a thought.

We say we need innovators in our world and we say we need 21st-century learners and problem solvers, but I ask you, "What does this mean?" Standard curriculum is not enough, never will be enough EVEN with Common Core! Too often, parents of gifted kids will start a conversation in schools with "I'm not trying to be one of those parents, but . . ." It is as though they are ashamed to advocate for their own kids. Be brave and speak up! How can we truly educate these wonderful minds if the conversation itself makes us quiet?

Tracey Hosey, Director of Gifted Education and
parent of gifted children, Yorkville, IL

ON MESSING UP A FREE LUNCH

Four states have yet to adopt the CCSS, with concerns regarding everything from potential costs, questionable effectiveness (just because educators *say* the CCSS will raise achievement, what proof do they have?), and the states' rights to do what they darn well please when it comes to educating their children. In advocating for her state's autonomy, Governor Nikki Haley of South Carolina, which adopted the CCSS under a former governor's reign, said she believes that "just as we should not relinquish control of education to the Federal government, nor should we cede it to the consensus of the other states" (Birch, 2012, para. 6). To which the U.S. Department of Education Secretary Arne Duncan responded that Haley's fear of losing control of schools is "a conspiracy theory in search of a conspiracy" (Vander-Hart, 2012, para. 3). The state of Texas, likewise, will not adopt the CCSS, using the rationale that its state-level standards are revised every 10 years, and because the most recent revision was in 2009, the State Board of Education is quite satisfied with the Lone Star State's progress in this area. Nebraska and Virginia (two other holdouts) have a mishmash of their own concerns. Still, it is pretty remarkable that 46 State Boards of Education can agree on *anything* this quickly.

But wait, there's more! The next set of national standards to be adopted is in the area of science, called the Next Generation Science Standards (see http://www.nextgenscience.org). If you think it was a maelstrom in states like South Carolina when it came to standards that dealt with Shakespeare and Pythagoras, can you imagine the hues and cries when science standards that raise the specters of climate change and evolution come up for adoption? The Luddites are likely to come out in full force when these "theories" are announced as being scientific enough in origin that our children should learn about them in school.

And just for good measure, here is another instance of how the CCSS were to get metaphorically short-sheeted by some administrators who are obviously ignorant of the needs of gifted kids. In the Wake County, NC, schools, elementary-age students were to no longer be allowed to take middle school math courses, because of the belief that the CCSS in math will be so rigorous that no elementary student could possibly handle the content of sixth-grade math (Kristof, 2012). At the time of this announcement, the decision seemed a bit premature, considering that the Common Core math standards had yet to be implemented for even one school year. A lawsuit was filed on behalf of a fifth-grade girl who would now need to repeat fifth-grade math, even though she'd already passed a middle school level math course of greater difficulty.

"It wouldn't be your mothers or father's or grandfather's Algebra I," school official Rodney Trice said in defense of this ludicrous policy decision (Kristof, 2012, para. 9).

Not long after, common sense prevailed—after a major outcry from parents and educators—and the Deputy Superintendent of Wake County schools, Cathy Moore, announced that the errant policy position had been reversed. Let us hope that this perfect example of messing up a free lunch, where the victims who are getting eaten are gifted kids, will not be repeated anywhere else.

So what is the bottom line on how or if the CCSS will impact the learning of gifted children? At this point, the question remains unanswered, as it does for the impact of CCSS on education as a whole. Many proponents agree with Timothy Shanahan's view in an interestingly titled article called "The Common Core Ate My Baby (and Other Urban Legends)" that

> educators who shrug off these changes will face a harsh reality. The CCSS are significantly higher than what we're used to . . . we can either shift our practices now in response to these new, demanding standards—or we can wait until our communities find out how well we're *really* doing. (p. 16)

However, some equally-as-ardent detractors have proposed a point of view that should not be ignored:

> Some think (the CCSS) is progress. We don't. We think it deflects energy away from opportunities for building a collegial professional culture aimed at real teaching and learning. We think education is facing a crisis. The question is, can we emerge from this crisis with a renewed focus on real teaching and learning

and a wholesale rejection of standardization? (Grennon Brooks & Dietz, 2012, p. 65)

As newscasters are prone to say to tease you to watch their broadcasts, "details at 11."

ONTO ANOTHER REALITY

The preceding discussion of panaceas that aren't might make a thinking person feel very discouraged. It seems that no matter what "innovation" comes down the pike to improve education for all students, "all" does not include gifted kids. Perhaps that oft-stated bromide that "gifted kids are smart . . . they'll be fine" is at play here. The reality is . . . that bromide is sometimes true: Even without attention paid to their unique intellectual and emotional needs, many gifted kids succeed in school and in life. It just seems to me that an approach to meeting their needs should be more targeted and less scattershot. Are we willing to leave to chance the well-being of millions of gifted kids whose lives would certainly be enhanced by direct attention being paid to their minds and hearts? In more than a few of our United States, the sad answer is yes, as gifted students lie on the sacrificial altar of school reform.

CHAPTER 6

LEGISLATIVE ABSURDITY . . .

AND THE ORGANIZATIONS THAT TRY TO REIN IT IN

magine this scenario: You are the parent of a child with a severe learning disability and the school that your child attends is doing a great job in providing instructional accommodations to address your kid's unique learning needs. Then, a job relocation requires you to move to another state and when you approach the principal of the new school your child will be attending, you are told that they do not have services for kids with disabilities. Perhaps the money isn't there, or maybe the school district has a philosophy that disabled kids will do just fine if placed in a regular classroom. "Besides, when you really think about it, doesn't *everyone* have some type of learning disability or another?" the principal asks you. "We need to learn to make do with whatever other talents we possess, don't we?"

If you received this response, your next stop would likely be to an attorney's office, as school districts are *required* to offer assistance to students with a professionally diagnosed handicapping condition that impairs their learning. The services may vary from school to school, but some level of educational intervention is mandated by federal law. No U.S. school district can just walk away from a child with a disability and say to the parents, "Sorry, we have no responsibility to address your child's unique needs."

Sadly, this scenario is encountered by parents of gifted children *every day of every year*, for the federal government has never mandated that gifted children be provided anything other than FAPE—a **F**ree and **A**ppropriate **P**ublic **E**ducation. And because FAPE does not guarantee an optimal education, just an "appropriate" one, gifted children's learning needs are generally addressed or ignored at a school district's discretion.

In the 2012–2013 *State of the Nation in Gifted Education* report (NAGC, 2013), disturbing data are presented about the lack of cohesiveness—and downright neglect—of gifted children's needs in many locales. Here are some examples of the widespread inconsistencies of how gifted children are dealt with across America:

◇ Fourteen states provide no funding to local school districts to serve gifted students.

◇ Of the 25 states that provide funds to school districts, 9 states provided funding of less than $10 million statewide. Only eight states provided $40 million or more.

◇ Although the majority of states have laws and policies that require school districts to identify and serve their highly able students, most of the policies are partially or totally unfunded. Indeed, only four states fully fund these obligations.

◇ Only three states require preservice teachers to have any training in how to work with gifted children in a classroom setting.

◇ Only 17 states require teachers hired to work with gifted students to have a gifted education teaching credential.

◇ Only 22 states have one or more full-time employees at their State Department of Education assigned to work on behalf of gifted children; 20 states have less than a full-time professional in this role.

◇ Only nine states have policies permitting acceleration of students; 22 states leave these decisions to local districts.

◇ Sixteen states prohibit children from entering kindergarten early and three states disallow middle school students from being dual-enrolled in high school courses

◇ Only nine states report on the academic performance and/or learning growth of gifted students as a separate group on the state report cards.

These and other data paint a picture that is as confusing as it is bleak. Not only do policies about gifted children vary greatly from state to state, but even *within* a single state. So, a child might be identified as gifted in Dearborn, but not in Detroit; in Wisconsin, but not West Virginia. And a teacher of the gifted in one state might have a master's degree specializing in this population, while in another state, the gifted kids are assigned to a teacher with little knowledge about or interest in teaching them.

Could you imagine the outcry if a teacher was allowed to teach AP Calculus without having a math background? Or if the state director of early childhood education had only taught at the high school level? Such absurdities would not be tolerated in most areas of education, but in gifted education, such absurdities are more the norm than the exception.

Between 2011–2014, not a single federal education dollar has been appropriated by Congress specifically for addressing the needs of gifted children. Yet, this is the same set of Congresspeople who decry our standing in the world when it comes to educational attainment in math and science; the same Congresspeople who worry about the "achievement gap" between high-ability minority and low-income students when compared to their nonminority counterparts; the same Congresspeople who worry that other nations will surpass America in business and industry within a decade. Talking a good game about needing to grow America's next generation of entrepreneurs and big thinkers while sitting on their collective hands when it comes to providing even a modicum of financial support for gifted children, Congress is guilty of widespread doublespeak: They say one thing and do another.

ENOUGH BLAME TO GO AROUND

The federal government is not the only entity that shirks its responsibility when it comes to addressing the needs of gifted children. As the data presented on the previous pages attest, many states also do a fine job of botching up the works, as well. Let's start with the basics: the definition of giftedness. In a study published by McClain and Pfeiffer (2012), it was found that 48 states define giftedness in some way (Massachusetts and South Dakota do not). Some states categorize "gifted" as a separate entity, while others are more expansive and use "gifted and talented." Twenty-four states have changed their definition of giftedness in the past decade, with at least one, Indiana, switching to the more politically correct term of "high ability." Forty-five states use "intelligence" as a criterion for giftedness (which begs the question, "What do the other states use?"), and 39 states add achievement into the mix. Only 27 states include "creativity" in their state definition and 15 states include "leadership skills," even as Georgia eliminated leadership from its definition recently.

Reading all of these data brings to mind the tale of the seven blind men trying to describe an elephant. Because each man touched only one part of the elephant—the trunk, the tail, the rough skin—there was no agreement on what the pachyderm actually looked like. Looks pretty much the same with the definition of giftedness, doesn't it?

However, because there is more overlap than disagreement within most state definitions of giftedness, I could live with the subtle distinctions—if not for this: How giftedness gets *identified* often has little to do with how it is *defined*. In an analysis of McClain and Pfeiffer's data, Scott Barry Kaufman (2012) questioned the validity of many identification approaches. For example, although most states used a "multiple criteria" approach to giftedness, in which no one test score qualifies or disqualifies someone as gifted, 16 states reported that they "do not require, recommend, or adhere to any one specific criterion for identifying gifted students" (p. 2). It seems that in these states, whimsy rules the day when it comes to which kid is gifted and which one is not. And remember those 27 states that used the word "creativity" in defining giftedness? Of these, only 9 states used any type of creativity test or measurement to locate it in a child. Kaufman also decried the fixation on identifying giftedness just once, and never again considering if the label has been applied (or *not* applied) to a youngster appropriately. He wrote, "no schools explicitly include provisions to constantly re-test all students . . . Unfortunately, this is the opposite of what the latest research shows about the malleability and ongoing development of different areas of expertise" (p. 2).

The bottom line is this: Without a cohesive definition of what *any* phenomenon is—in this case, giftedness—the likelihood of inequity abounds. Something tells me that if a kid *is* gifted in Dearborn then she also is in Detroit—and even across the state line in Columbus. Coming to grips with this 50-state approach to defining a common term is the first step to cohesion for this disparate field of study.

AND THE WINNER IS!

Texas: for absurdity.

The Lone Star State is known for doing things big, including making a huge, awful decision recently that affects the learning of every child in the state. As part of the 2012 Republican Party platform, the planks dealing with education call for the following (Strauss, 2012):

◇ an opposition to the teaching of critical thinking in public schools, as such instruction has "the purpose of challenging the student's fixed beliefs and undermining parental authority" (para. 2);

◇ an end to any instruction in the area of multiculturalism, as "we favor strengthening our common American identity and loyalty instead of political correctness that nurtures alienation among racial and ethnic groups" (para. 13);

◇ instruction in "theories such as life origins and environmental change [that] should be taught as challengeable scientific theories subject to change as new data is [sic] produced" (para. 20);

◇ the dismantling of mandatory pre-kindergarten and kinder-garten programs, saying "we urge Congress to repeal govern-ment-sponsored programs that deal with early childhood education" (para. 21); and

◇ the dismantling of school health care medical clinics, except in higher education.

It's hard to believe that the folks who sponsored these and other ideas (they also decry sex education and believe that corporal punishment in schools is "effective and legal") believe they are educating children for the 21st century, not the 19th. This political platform on education was roundly ridiculed by many—including Stephen Colbert—so the Republican Party Communications Director backpedaled a bit and said that "critical thinking" wasn't supposed to be included in the platform as an evil undermining of parental authority. But since it is in the platform, and the process to take it out requires approval at another party convention that won't soon be held, Texas is still a place where teaching kids how to see multiple sides of an issue and demanding that they back up their opinions with evidence are not welcomed. Perhaps billboards welcoming people to the state as they enter from Oklahoma or New Mexico should contain this slogan: "Welcome to Texas! Where Ignorance Is Bliss!"

Even though gifted children are not mentioned directly in this party platform of ludicrous ideas, they will certainly be impacted negatively by them, as will their teachers. And because both houses of the Texas State Legislature and the Governor's Office have been ruled by Republicans for more than a decade, these ideas are not just words on paper—they translate into policy.

Yes, every other state probably has some wacky policies and laws that impact negatively on gifted children, but it seems to me that it's hard to top Texas for overall ineptitude.

ASSOCIATIONS THAT SUPPORT GIFTED CHILDREN: ANOTHER AVALANCHE OF ACRONYMS

Advocacy takes many forms and, when it comes to supporting the needs of gifted children, it apparently also takes many associations with overlapping goals to make things happen.

The most prominent organization dedicated to the gifted child population is the National Association for Gifted Children. Founded in 1954 by Ann Isaacs, a preschool director from Ohio who saw even young children beginning to underachieve, Isaacs led the organization for a quarter century. Isaacs published and edited the organization's *Gifted Child Quarterly* (*GCQ*) publication from 1957–1975 (even today, *GCQ* is the flagship journal of NAGC). The author of more than 250 articles herself (as well as a noted musician and composer), Isaacs left NAGC in 1975 to start a different organization, the National Association for Creative Children and Adults, which did not go on to achieve the success of NAGC. Ann Isaacs' extensive collection of personal and professional memorabilia—everything from advertising brochures for IQ tests to an article she wrote on religious education for gifted children—are archived at the University of Cincinnati.

Today, NAGC is based in Washington, DC, and has approximately 7,000 members. Although its many publications cover a broad array of issues of interest to parents and educators, the main audience for its efforts is teachers and administrators who work with gifted children. The annual NAGC conference features noted scholars from the gifted education world and attracts approximately 3,000 participants each year. The move to Washington was predicated on the belief that being in the "associational hub" of DC would allow NAGC officers to interact with related educational organizations and apprise them of the needs of gifted kids. This is yet to happen, as NAGC pretty much functions as its own little island of advocacy.

Just up the road a bit, in Virginia, lie the offices of the Council for Exceptional Children (CEC), the juggernaut of associations that advocate for children with special needs, including gifted kids. Begun in 1922 by Teachers' College professor Elizabeth Ferrell and her graduate students, CEC went from 400 members in 1926 to more than 30,000 members today. Composed of divisions that deal with the many different areas of exceptionality, CEC's branch that deals with gifted children is called The Association for the Gifted (TAG). A lesser force than NAGC, TAG does not have its own conference (it is a small player at the annual CEC conference) and its publications are fewer. The one area where TAG excels that NAGC does not is in the realm of federal legislation that could affect gifted kids. With CEC's clout of 30,000 members, they have a presence and a voice on Capitol Hill that NAGC has never been able to harness. (I'm sure the NAGC leaders would take exception to this observation; so be it.) Still, as mentioned in an earlier chapter, most federal efforts (and dollars) that apply to special education omit any mention of gifted kids, and this has not changed much over the decades. CEC's main focus has never been gifted kids—and it never will be. You might say CEC is an advocacy group for gifted kids in name only.

The third major organization has a much different focus—and much different origins—than either NAGC or CEC. Supporting Emotional Needs of the Gifted (SENG) began out of tragedy. In 1980, 16-year-old Dallas Egbert, a highly gifted young man already in college, committed suicide. When his parents went searching for answers, they approached psychologist James Webb at Wright State University in Ohio. To their collective surprise, they could find no organization whose primary focus was the social and emotional development of gifted individuals. Invited to tell their son's story on the then-popular Phil Donahue Show, Dallas' parents voiced their frustration with having no place to turn to seek help for their son or themselves. After that TV show's airing, NAGC received more than 20,000 letters and calls from parents whose concerns were similar to the Egbert's. Seeing such a profound need going unaddressed, James Webb began SENG in 1981—and it's been going strong ever since.

SENG's primary focus is the full human development of gifted children *and adults*. Appropriate educational placement is one element of this development, but not its sole one. The primary recipients of SENG's services are parents of gifted kids, noted most obviously by its annual summer conference. And, just to show that SENG is true to its mission, it even runs a parallel conference for gifted children. Unlike NAGC and CEC, SENG doesn't just talk *about* gifted kids, it talks *with* them.

There are several other smaller national organizations advocating for gifted children: the American Association for Gifted Children (AAGC), based at Duke University, is the most notable; the Institute for Educational Advancement, mentioned earlier, is an association that sponsors the Caroline D. Bradley Scholarship and other programs for gifted children; and virtually every state and Canadian province has a locally based counterpart that affiliates with one or more of the "Big 3" highlighted above. Still, despite all of the combined efforts of these associations, the reason cited for founding the AAGC in 1946—gifted children being the "most neglected children in our democracy"—is still problematic today.

Having served as President of TAG, having been on the Board of Directors of NAGC for 9 years, having been Co-Director of SENG in the mid-1980s, and serving now on the Board of Directors of IEA, I believe I have a balanced perspective of what each of these associations offers. And if I had to place my hope and trust in any of these organizations moving the world of the gifted child forward in a more positive direction, I'd put my money on SENG. Its focus is sharp, clear, national in scope, and as apolitical as any association can be these days. Also, because the main recipients of its products and services are parents and kids, each member brings in a personal stake to the conversation about what's best for the gifted people in our midst.

I'd like to see the three largest of these associations—SENG, NAGC, and TAG—get along and play nicely with the others, but I believe strongly that that is not going to happen to any great extent. The "Three P's"—politics, personality, and pride—prevent true collaboration from taking place. I hope sincerely that I am wrong.

TIME TO MOVE ON

As this chapter comes to an end, you might be shaking your head wondering if all hope is lost for gifted kids in America. School policies (. . . or lack thereof) impact gifted students and set them back rather than push them forward. The lack of uniformity of how (or if) to serve gifted students in schools makes for a crazy-quilt of practices that provide, at best, a disjointed education for our most capable students. And even some of the better ideas and programs discussed in earlier chapters—Advanced Placement, STEM schools, enrichment programs in elementary grades—come complete with their own flaws.

So let's end this chapter on a positive note, one that has us reflecting on just what is possible to advance the cause of gifted education in America. How's this for wisdom?

The bright do take care of themselves, to the extent that they seldom become financially dependent on society at large or otherwise socially burdensome. However, this is scarcely an ideal of development for a far-seeing society.

What is needed for the support and development of these children . . . is what we may call a revolving foundation. By this I meant a fund from which the gifted young could draw at any age the means for their development, with the moral (not legal) obligation to repay according to ability to do so, after 20 years, without interest. By this plan the superior could invest in themselves; very little money would actually be spent, because it would come back again, and the nation would benefit in ways not yet fully foreseeable. It would be a great experiment in social science.

What the gifted child needs is an education that will challenge his interest, will utilize his power of learning to the fullest, and will constitute a genuine opportunity for mental development.

What forward-thinking ideas, wouldn't you say? And the vibrancy of these observations is as current today as when they were written—in 1931 and 1938. Yes, it is the timeless wisdom of Leta Hollingworth, reincarnated in a recent article (Schultz, 2011, p. 16), to which we must adhere if we are to see the lives of gifted children improve. The following chapter will provide a roadmap as to which directions we need to take, but the architect of the road itself, Leta Hollingworth, lived more than a century ago.

CHAPTER 7

WHAT NEXT?

GIFTED CHILDREN'S BILL OF RIGHTS

You have a right . . .

1. to learn about your giftedness.
2. to learn something new every day.
3. to be passionate about your talent area without apologies.
4. to have an identity beyond your talent area.
5. to feel good about your accomplishments.
6. to make mistakes.
7. to seek guidance in the development of your talent.
8. to have multiple peer groups and a variety of friends.
9. to choose which of your talent areas you wish to pursue.
10. not to be gifted at everything.

(Siegle, 2007)

It's hardly rocket science: the only thing gifted kids want is what their advocates fight for—a life filled with purpose, an education that matters, and friends who take them seriously. The above "Gifted Children's Bill of Rights" is neither controversial nor unrealistic. So far, however, it's been unrealized.

In this chapter, I will present a variety of suggestions for improving the lot of America's gifted children in its public schools. Some of the ideas will be specific to gifted education itself, while others will require some more systemic changes in public policy. Taken together, they will provide some needed direction to a field in desperate need of a course correction. Sailing as we now are in a sea of conflicting practices, gifted children and their advocates deserve something better, something more substantial, than occasional bursts of educational excellence.

This chapter is divided into three distinct sections related to particular aspects of gifted education:

1. establishing a cohesive definition of giftedness,
2. adopting legitimate and sensible identification practices, and
3. implementing innovative and comprehensive programming practices.

Although I will cite research done by colleagues that addresses each of these areas, the final determination as to what seems best to advance the field of gifted education comes from a decidedly biased source: myself. With 35+ years of working with and for gifted children, teens, parents, and educators to back up my assertions, I feel pretty comfortable with my own voice of experience. If others wish to disagree with me—and I have no doubt they shall—let them write their own books. Ready? Let's move on.

ESTABLISHING A COHESIVE DEFINITION OF GIFTEDNESS

Perhaps no one put it better than Françoys Gagné, a professor of gifted child education hailing from Canada, in trying to determine what this sticky wicket called giftedness is all about. In his well-regarded Differentiated Model of Giftedness and Talent (DMGT; Gagné, 2004), he made a clear distinction between *giftedness,* which he cited as the possession of outstanding natural abilities, and *talents*, which are the exceptional mastery of developed abilities. Gagné's (2003) exact definition of giftedness and talent is:

> Giftedness designates the possession and use of untrained and spontaneously expressed natural abilities (called aptitudes or gifts), in at least one ability domain, to a degree that places an individual among

the top 10% of age peers. Talent designates the superior mastery of systematically developed abilities (or
skills) and places an individual within the top 10% of
age peers who are (or have been) active in that field.
(p. 67)

In clarifying the difference between giftedness and talent, Gagné
presupposed that genetics has something to do with giftedness, a belief
that gets debased with each new book published on the everyday nature
of genius. Also, by seeing giftedness as related to talent, *yet remaining
as a distinct entity*, Gagné broke down giftedness into several domains:

◇ *Intellectual*: fluid reasoning abilities like critical thinking,
memory, verbal and spatial abilities, and judgment, among
other attributes;

◇ *Creative*: imagination, originality, and inventiveness;

◇ *Socioaffective*: perceptiveness, empathy, leadership, and per-
suasiveness; and

◇ *Sensorimotor*: strengths in each of the five senses, plus motor
strength as noted through endurance and coordination.

One does not need to possess each of these characteristics in
abundance, but each attribute does need to be considered when the term
gifted is ascribed to a particular child. Once these factors are found to a
high degree within an individual, Gagné proposed that certain catalysts
will propel him forward into the development of talent. These catalysts
might be *intrapersonal*—for example, an individual's temperament
and desire to push forward in his learning—or *environmental*, such as
events or people apart from the gifted individual who give guidance
and experiences that cause the person to move from potential to
fruition. The resultant talents that could emerge span all dimensions
of human activity: academics, sports, the arts, business, and more. An
interesting adjunct to Gagné's definition of giftedness is his inclusion
of the element of "chance" into the equation. So if you happen to be
a highly verbal individual living in a culture where few people care
about the spoken word, then the likelihood of your being noticed as

exceptional is quite low. This inclusion of chance brings in an intriguing "right time, right place" wrinkle to the definition of giftedness.

The biggest benefit of Gagné's definition is its multipart exploration of an entity that is as complex as it is broad: giftedness. Further, it is one of the few conceptions of giftedness that ties together its natural occurrence in some individuals with its development as an identifiable talent. The key words in his definition of giftedness—"the possession and use of untrained and spontaneously expressed natural abilities"—allows Gagné's work to transcend those of others who wish to dismiss giftedness in people who do not take their natural abilities seriously enough to capitalize on them. Yes, a person *can* be gifted and not show it through his schoolwork as a child or his life work as an adult. Gagné's respect for individual choice when it comes to deciding whether or not to perform at exceptional levels is singular among definitions of giftedness.

If only it had one additional element to it . . .

ENTER THE CAVALRY

For reasons that are probably obvious, educator types like Gagné's definitions of giftedness and talent. Why? Because they capture the connection between what a child comes equipped with, intellectually speaking, and what teachers can do to bring this giftedness to fruition. As Gagné has often stated, tongue firmly in cheek, "talent development is a process in search of a product."

However, there is one important element of Gagné's definition of giftedness that is not prominent: the enhanced emotional development that often accompanies high intelligence. To satisfy this aspect of a gifted child's life, we need to turn elsewhere.

The first place to look for a conception of giftedness that focuses on the nonacademic parts of a gifted person's life is the work of Annemarie Roeper. First, a bit of her background: Annemarie was cofounder (with her husband, George) of the Roeper School in Michigan in 1941. Philosophically aligned with the idea that the goal of all education is self-actualization within an interdependent world, the Roepers decided to focus their school's attention on gifted children exclusively beginning in 1956. The school grew from a small entity for young children to its current two-campus, 600+ student body of gifted kids from nursery school through grade 12. Having worked with gifted children for more than 65 years(!), Annemarie Roeper saw time and time again how gifted children morph into gifted adults, encountering along the way both some powerful triumphs and some devastating defeats.

In 1982, Roeper forged a definition of giftedness that arose from her multiple decades of work with gifted individuals. Here it is:

> Giftedness is a greater awareness, a greater sensitivity, and a greater ability to understand and transform perceptions into intellectual and emotional experiences. (p. 21)

I'm not sure what amazes me more about this definition—its simplicity or its depth. However, I do know this: Whenever parents of gifted kids hear this definition, they almost universally think, "This describes my kid." Unlike most other definitions of giftedness that focus on the gifted individual's usefulness to society, Roeper's definition addresses directly the inner experiences and emotional vulnerability of the gifted individual, something that parents of gifted kids experience on a daily basis. The qualities that Roeper highlighted—the greater awareness and sensitivity that gifted individuals possess—is what propels them to see the world from a different vantage point than many around them. These kids (and adults) simply experience life in a higher key, and they understand that although it's not always politically correct to tell people that the guy behind the curtain in Emerald City is not a wizard but merely a man, they feel compelled to make the obvious known. As Roeper (1991) wrote:

> Gifted individuals do not know what creates the drive, the energy, the absolute necessity to act. They may have no choice but to explore, compose, write, paint, develop theories . . . research or do whatever else it is that has become uppermost in their minds.

They need to know; they need to learn; they need to
climb the mountain because it is there. (p. 90)

This definition of giftedness is a transformative shift from its
number-laden, percentile-driven counterparts that address only one
part of a gifted child's life: the mind. Roeper's definition leaves room
for individuality among this group of children and adults clustered
under the label of gifted.

Gagné's and Roeper's definitions are not competitive but, rather,
complementary. The bridge that can unite them comes with the last
definition of giftedness I'll highlight, one that focuses on a quality
called *asynchronous development.*

Imagine this scenario: A child with the body of a 14-year-old has
the mental capacity of an 8-year-old. Certainly, in such a situation, the
boy or girl would receive special attention in school and at home to
address the wide developmental discrepancies that exist. Now, reverse
the scenario: a child with the body of an 8-year-old has the mental
abilities of a 14-year-old. A developmental discrepancy just as wide,
yet this child—a gifted child—may not get any special attention at all.
He or she might simply be expected to exist happily in a third-grade
classroom that is as bad and uncomfortable a fit as was O. J.'s famous
courtroom glove.

The situation above was cited by gifted advocate Linda Silverman
(minus the O. J. analogy) as a poignant and relevant example of the
need to provide gifted children with an education commensurate
with their various developmental needs. It also led her and several
colleagues—the "Columbus Group," so named because of the Ohio
city where they met—to formulate a definition of giftedness worth
noting. Here's how giftedness is defined as asynchronous development
(AD; Morelock, 1992):

> Giftedness is asynchronous development in which
> cognitive abilities and heightened intensity combine
> to create experiences and awareness that are quali-
> tatively different from the norm. This asynchrony
> increases with higher intellectual capacity. The

uniqueness of the gifted renders them particularly vulnerable and requires modifications in parenting, teaching, and counseling in order to develop optimally.

If you note a good degree of overlap between this definition and the one put forth by Annemarie Roeper, you'd be correct. Silverman was one of Roeper's greatest friends and colleagues and this AD conception of giftedness fleshes out the Roeper definition by telling folks what they need to do to address the AD that is so common in gifted children. As Silverman (n.d.) explained, this AD increases as the gifted child's intellect rises, meaning that the "recipe" for serving gifted children properly in school, and understanding them at home, will call for different amounts of ingredients for the particular gifted child in question. Thus, for a child whose discrepancy between physical age and intellect is just one year, a pinch of curriculum modification may be needed, whereas for a child whose physical/mental discrepancy is 4 years, that pinch turns into a cupful.

Another group of children who benefit from this AD view of giftedness is the 2E children mentioned in an earlier chapter of this book. Because many gifted kids with disabilities have learning styles and preferences that don't mesh with typical school lessons—for example, many of them have a visual-spatial orientation along with weaknesses in reading, writing, spelling, and calculation—this definition speaks directly to the inherent vulnerability of these gifted children placed in a school environment that is misaligned with their many, often hidden, strengths.

Further, Silverman (n.d.) believed that the view of giftedness she espouses is one that will be more readily accepted by educators and legislators. Listen to her logic:

> The concept of giftedness as asynchrony is useful in attempting to gain support for the gifted, as most other definitions equate giftedness with high achievement. Special programs often sound like more advantages for an already-advantaged group. The perennial

concern about elitism is bypassed by adopting this perspective . . . It is a way of viewing giftedness as a set of qualitative differences that need to be addressed at home and at school. (para. 9)

This AD view of giftedness has been embraced by many in the gifted community, especially those who believe that gifted children are more than just the sum of their achievements. However, its nonquantitative nature means that it is unlikely to be selected by a school district or state looking to identify gifted children for special services. Thus, here's my suggestion: As a society, let us accept two visions of giftedness. The first one, which can guide programmatic decisions at the local and state level, is Gagné's DMGT model, which unites a definition with school services that could be offered to gifted children. Secondly, the AD definition can be used more often by psychologists, who attempt to find giftedness in both its most blatant and hidden forms; by frontline educators, who question why tried-and-true teaching strategies that usually work with gifted children do not work for a particular gifted child; and by parents, as they attempt to understand and cope with a gifted child who is 10 years old chronologically, 13 years old intellectually, emotionally mature beyond years, and socially adept only around adults.

The field of gifted education has been monkeying around with the definition of giftedness almost since its inception, doggedly determined to find one conception of giftedness that will fit everyone. Folks, That's. Not. Going. To. Happen. Let's just try to get comfortable with the reality that the two definitions I propose here are sufficient to envelop the vast majority of gifted individuals that come our way in our lifetimes. The wheel has already been invented. Now, let's put it to good use.

ADOPTING LEGITIMATE AND SENSIBLE IDENTIFICATION PRACTICES

A middle school English teacher I know from Texas relates how she was trying to get her students to recall some elements used in writing that made their stories more interesting and varied. One student suggested the use of "onomatopoeia," a word the teacher found difficult to spell as she wrote it on the whiteboard. A second writing technique named by a student was "irony," and when the teacher asked for someone to define irony, a usually disengaged eighth grader in the back of the room offered this: "Irony is an English teacher who doesn't know how to spell onomatopoeia."

Is this a gifted child? More than likely!

If I were told that I was unable to use any paper-and-pencil instruments to determine whether or not a child was gifted, I'd be fine with that. All I'd need is to ask a child to tell me his or her favorite joke or pun, as the eighth grader above did spontaneously with the onomatopoeia/irony example. However, such informal methods to identify giftedness are probably not going to be used any time soon, as their legitimacy is suspect due to the lack of a precise number that

Traditionally underrepresented in gifted programs, Black, Hispanic, and Native American students are discriminated against in schools across our nation, having limited access to services that meet their intellectual, academic, creative, and affective needs. Historically, the families of these groups have long histories of valuing education and surviving across generations, even in the midst of oppressive conditions. Improving family engagement among culturally different groups and valuing their roles as educational advocacy partners will help erase discriminatory practices in gifted education, enhance the cultural competency of educators, and increase the likelihood that all gifted students, regardless of their race and culture, will reach their highest potential.

Joy Lawson Davis, Professor of Education,
Virginia Union University, Richmond, VA

either qualifies or disqualifies someone from being identified as gifted. A shame, really, and therein lies the rub with gifted identification: Precision often overrides common sense and observation.

Go ahead: Ask a gifted coordinator, "What is the most challenging aspect of your job?" and it is highly likely that "student identification" would be at or near the top of the list. Gone are the days when a high IQ alone was sufficient enough information to qualify a child as gifted. Today, in a school population as diverse culturally and economically as any time in our history, identification of gifted students has become almost mythically difficult.

The security once felt by an IQ of 140+ is now under scrutiny— not so much for the students who earn such a high score, but for those who don't. It's not that we're so concerned about the "false positives"— no one scores a 142 IQ by accident—but rather, the "false negatives": kids who score lower on standardized tests, including IQ tests, than their daily academic performance and/or intellectual demeanor would suggest. There's also the question of achievement: What happens when you have a child who scores at the 98th percentile on standardized tests of language arts and mathematics, but whose classroom grades are barely passing? And what about the increasing number of students who enter our schools with just a nascent command of the English language—how do we measure their abilities appropriately? Given these and other wrinkles, student identification for gifted programs often causes those in charge of doing so to constantly look at their efforts as merely adequate, not sufficient. It's not who they *do* identify that causes sleepless nights for gifted coordinators, it's the kids they *don't* identify.

Perhaps, if gifted identification was done systematically instead of being a one-size-fits-all, once-a-year procedure, things would improve. Maybe if gifted identification was linked to the kinds of services that gifted children would receive subsequent to their identification, rather than as a mere exercise that might or might not align with the educational services that follow, less stress would be involved in the process. And who knows? If we fessed up and acknowledged that gifted identification is as much art as it is science, requiring finesse and individualization instead of a dogmatic approach with no wiggle room, all would be well. So let's see how we can add some sanity to a process that need not be as schizophrenic as it often is.

We'll examine three key elements in gifted identification in our quest to identify gifted kids the right way:

1. *when* to identify
2. *whom* to identify
3. *how* to identify

Even though each of these three elements should be perceived as a whole, investigating them separately for the sake of clarity will be done here. Let's begin.

WHEN TO IDENTIFY

It can be argued that we seldom identify gifted children; instead, they identify themselves to us. When a child is using multisyllabic words (like "multisyllabic") in proper context as a 5-year-old, or is developing apps for her iPhone at age 9, or is capable of holding intelligent conversations with adults at the age of 7, the tests we would give to assess these strengths seldom *identify* giftedness as much as they *validate* what careful observation already tells us: that a particular child is thinking and acting light years ahead of typical expectations.

This raises the essential question of timing: Do we wait until school begins for a child to qualify him or her as gifted, or do we do so at the earliest time we can? Nancy Robinson (1993), a scholar who has researched this issue for decades, is a big fan of "earlier is better," finding that children identified as gifted in preschool and kindergarten maintained their heightened abilities throughout their school years. Likewise, Annemarie Roeper was a staunch advocate of gifted identification at as young an age as possible. Using a method she devised called "Qualitative Assessment" (more on its specifics in a subsequent section), Roeper (2007) believed that by observing and reacting to a great variety of clues, the assessor of giftedness in young children can use her intuitive abilities to form an overall impression of the young gifted child. Further, Harrison (2003) found that the young gifted child's search for "complexity and connection," qualities often noticed first by parents and preschool educators, can be reliable indicators of giftedness.

Unfortunately, it is the exception rather than the rule for schools to identify giftedness in young children. Operating under the misguided belief that 4-year-olds are still so malleable that putting such a lasting label as "gifted" on them is too heavy a burden, districts often defer gifted identification until second, third, or fourth grade. However, in doing so, they are missing out on what are perhaps the most golden years of the intellect—a time when kids are still learning for its own sake, not to snatch a grade that will earn accolades and rewards from adults. Based on the myth that even the smartest kids will "even out" by third grade, when other students will catch up to the gifted ones due to their school experiences, identification is delayed. But . . . identification delayed means appropriate educational services withheld, leaving young gifted children in classrooms that do not take full advantage of their heightened intellects.

Imagine the reverse: If we suspected a child to have a disability of any type at age 4, we would not wait until several years later to begin to identify this child's specific needs and serve her appropriately. How absurd! However, this same level of absurdity is justified by some who wish to delay the identification of giftedness. Their fear? That somewhere down the line, we'll have to tell parents that a mistake was made; their child is not gifted after all.

And maybe that will happen, on occasion. Perhaps a young child who has been exposed to books at an early age and who lives in a household with parents who take great care to introduce said child to all of life's wonders, might be identified as gifted when, in fact, he is merely the recipient of good parenting. If heightened abilities are not innate but, instead, the result of frequent interaction with the wider world, then yes, the distinction between this child's academic achievements and those of other children of the same age might diminish over time. However, if the child in question has natural abilities that are *enhanced* by environmental factors but not *dependent* upon them to increase, the gifted label will, indeed, be valid.

Bottom line in identification is this: I would rather commit the sin of *commission* than *omission*. I would rather identify a young child as gifted and get appropriate educational services as early as I can, despite the possibility that I have overshot my target, than I would to ignore what appear to be innate signs of giftedness for the sake of greater certainty later on. Identifying a child as gifted as soon as the signs become obvious give this child's teachers the opportunity to finesse the curriculum to the child's advantage. Waiting until years later to identify giftedness risks the danger of stifling this child's learning and encouraging boredom and social or behavioral problems in the classroom. Better to err on the side of potential and identify giftedness as soon as we suspect it exists within a child.

Every label that can be applied to a child—gifted, disabled, athletic, musical, hyperactive, kind—should be considered a tentative one. Children, especially the youngest ones, are bound to change over time in every way possible that they can. Still, deferring the issuance of a label for fear of being wrong later on cannot be used as the basis for our decision making. As long as the child in question has been looked at carefully by individuals who know what to look for, a tentative label is better than no label it all. It gains access for the child to whatever educational or emotional services are necessary to enhance this individual development.

> *In a study completed by Bromberg and Theokas (2014), the researchers found that although high-achieving White, Black, and Latino students take similar course loads during high school, students from low-socioeconomic (SES) backgrounds take fewer advanced courses, and are less likely to take AP or IB options, than their more advantaged peers. This was true even for high-achieving students from low-SES families. Further, the percentage of high-achieving students who get a score of 3 or higher on AP tests (and therefore, may qualify for receiving college credit) varies by race: 36% for Black students, 51% for Latino students, and 68% for White students.*
>
> *When it comes to college admissions, high-achieving White students are more than twice as likely to take the ACT or SAT than their Black and Latino counterparts, and the pattern continues in the percentages of students who enter moderately or highly selective colleges: 41% of Latino students, 54% of Black students, and 67% of White students. Similarly, only 44% of low-SES high achievers enroll in moderately or highly selective colleges, as opposed to 78% of their more advantaged peers.*
>
> *Bromberg and Theokas (2014) concluded that:*
>
> > *low-SES students and students of color deserve better. It is up to schools and educators to equip students with the experiences, knowledge, skills, and attitudes that will put them in contention for postsecondary opportunities that can truly dislodge long-entrenched patterns in our society. (p. 22)*

WHOM TO IDENTIFY

How great would it be if every gifted child could be identified at age 3 or 4 with 100% precision! Alas, human development is not always even; likewise, human judgment is not always accurate. So we may find that a middle school's greatest slacker is actually a budding genius who succeeds everywhere but inside a classroom. Or, a breathtakingly talented musician is overlooked until someone shows her the magic and majesty of a piano. Perhaps a boy who struggles to read is seen as "dumb" until an observant someone notices that his level of comprehension when someone reads to him is as perceptive as someone twice his age. So yeah, as much as life would be fairer if the playing fields were even for everyone, human nature is such that our unique individualities sometimes make it difficult to be certain of who knows what at any given time. That's why gifted identification is not an *event*, it's a *process*.

The easiest kids to identify as gifted are the stereotypes: the smart kids who excel in school, speak politely to adults, and are eager to put their intellectual talents on display. Whether identified as gifted or not, this type of child often floats through school with few problems—she chooses high achievement as a personal goal and teachers are generally happy to accommodate this compliant kid with projects that are intellectually or creatively engaging. Ironically, although these types of gifted children are most likely to receive attention in school, they are probably the ones who need our help the least. Indeed, these are the gifted kids who make it through school well—with or without our help.

The gifted kids who remain under the radar are often the ones most in need of our collective attention. These are kids who "don't do school well" for a variety of reasons, from having a learning disability to simply being belligerent. Their achievement test scores show some marked instances of high ability but, because they are often coupled with some poor grades or behavioral issues, classroom teachers often recoil in disbelief that a kid "like that" can be gifted. It is a rare educator who can look beneath the veneer of mixed levels of achievement and see the giftedness that lies just below the surface.

If and when these kids are identified as gifted—which isn't often—the next hurdle they must overcome is adjusting to whatever gifted program components exist. For example, if you have a child identified as gifted who also struggles with dyslexia or dysgraphia, then a gifted program that is heavily verbal in nature, requiring students to produce an abundance of written output, will be a very bad match. Or if you have a gifted child who can take or leave school—and teachers—performing sporadically when the mood is right, many educators would not see this student as a strong gifted program candidate—at least not until such time that the student "buckles down" and achieves in the regular classroom assignments. Too, if you have a gifted child who is also diagnosed with Asperger's syndrome, group projects and class discussions might not just be unproductive, but downright painful for her.

School districts that seek to identify "difficult" gifted children like these are to be applauded for their efforts. However, the identification process is merely the first step, as the gifted program options that follow need to be tailored around both this child's gifts *and* struggles. If the match isn't good, it is no one's fault; it just needs to be fixed by trying multiple avenues to reach success. More on some possibilities later in this chapter.

Another category of gifted kid who is seldom identified is the "late bloomer." For whatever reasons—lack of English language skills, a family crisis that overrides concern about school, a medical condition that suppresses academic performance—some gifted children evade our detection due to no fault of their own. One of my students who comes to mind is Vitale, a boy who moved to the U.S. from Romania when he was a fifth grader. Little academic paperwork came with Vitale, and his parents' sketchy command of English made it difficult for us to get a clear picture of any of Vitale's latent academic strengths. Placed in a lower level class so that he wouldn't feel too much stress (a kind gesture but, in the long run, an erroneous one), Vitale languished through much of that year. However, by the onset of the following school year, Vitale's English skills had improved—it was the fourth language he had mastered—and as he became more comfortable with his emerging academic skills, Vitale became his own best advocate.

Never given more than basic math problems to solve, Vitale surprised us all by stating that he had already taken algebra in Romania—as a fourth grader. When allowed to prove his mastery on a comprehensive math exam, Vitale aced the test. When asked why he hadn't mentioned to anyone that he had such advanced math skills, Vitale responded that he assumed things were done differently in America—and he didn't want to appear rude and ask for something more challenging. Upon his high school graduation, Vitale was among the top 10 of his class, having taken virtually every advanced academic option that his school offered.

Sometimes, gifted student identification is little more than a formality, placing an IQ number on abilities that we assumed were there all along. And then there is Vitale, and countless others like him, who are hidden from our view until we take a closer look to find the extraordinary capabilities that are just waiting to be unleashed. The first step in doing so is the early and proper identification of *all types* of gifted kids, not just those who are the easiest ones to spot.

HOW TO IDENTIFY

Let me state something upfront about how to identify gifted children: It is an elaborate blend of quantitative data with qualitative intuition. Entire books are written on the identification process—what instruments to use, when to administer them, how to get valuable, anecdotal information from parents and teachers, using students to identify giftedness in classmates, etc.—yet a definitive process that guarantees perfect results remains elusive. So, rather than write yet another book on gifted student identification, I will focus here on some of the main tenets of the identification process. Because each school district has its own unique combination of preferred standardized tests and identification protocols, I won't get into a "this-test-is-better-than-that-test" scenario. Rather, I'll offer some time-proven pointers on doing the best job we can in making the imperfect world of gifted identification work to the advantage of kids who can benefit from our efforts.

Tenet #1: More data are not always preferable. If you are planning a vacation to Disney World from New York City, you can fly

138

there in 2 hours on a nonstop flight. But, if you live in Thermopolis, WY, your planning is a bit more difficult. The end goal is the same— getting to Orlando—but it'll take some extra work and planning to reach your goal. The same is true with gifted identification: If you have evidence that a child's IQ on a valid and reliable test is 144, you need look no further to determine if a child is gifted. However, if another child's IQ is 123, achievement test scores are high in math but average in verbal skills, and teachers give said child "mixed reviews" with regard to intellectual competence, then you'll need to dig a little deeper to determine if this child qualifies as gifted.

Gifted specialists often want to make the identification process as uniform as possible, which sounds like a laudable goal. However, when a single piece of information—an IQ of 144—is all that you need to pinpoint a child as gifted, time can be better spent looking for the "Thermopolis kids" whose path to the gifted label is not so clearly marked.

Consistency is important . . . except when it's not.

Katie's third-grade teacher agreed to let her test out of her spelling words and pick her own words as her "enrichment." Convinced Katie chose words too difficult, the teacher assumed that we must be coaching her. You should have seen me laugh one Friday afternoon: The teacher told Katie as we were leaving that on Monday she wanted her to spell "archaeobiology" backward, ". . . so work on that over the weekend." Katie took a step back, smiled, and retorted with "ygoloiboeahcra." That was the day her teacher finally realized she had an exceptional child in her class. That was the day she stopped trying to hold Katie back.

Jennifer Jenson, mother of gifted kids, crusader extraordinaire, Twinsburg, OH

Tenet #2: No one knows everything, everyone knows something. If you are looking to identify gifted children below the age of 6, it is silly to ignore the observations of their parents. If you wish to identify gifted kids in elementary school, the teachers who share 180 days a year with them are essential indicators of advanced abilities. And if your identification is taking place in middle or high school, why not ask the people who know these kids the best?: each other, using self-or peer nomination.

Of course, you may want to use some instruments that provide quantitative measures of a child's abilities, but test scores alone are insufficient. Consider this: Most tests are given within a day's time, often, just in an hour or 2. If, on test day, a child's abilities are masked by an empty belly, a head clogged with mucus, or a heart full of anxiety, it's unlikely that the child will achieve optimal performance. Standing by themselves, these test scores would not indicate gifted-level abilities; however, if these scores were just one piece of a bigger process that included observations from those who have seen the child develop over time, a more accurate assessment picture would emerge.

Allow me to let you in on a dirty little secret: In too many gifted programs, the goal of identification does not seem to be to locate as many gifted children as possible but rather, to find ways to eliminate candidates by finding a chink in their quantitative armor. This is another reason why we need to dig deeper to find gifted children who do not rise immediately to the surface by their evident brilliance.

Critics of using qualitative data will tell you all kinds of reasons why they don't work, claiming that the instruments themselves are flawed, that parents are naturally biased toward their own kids, that teachers will nominate only their high achievers, and that peers will select only their friends. Well, yes and no. If you simply do a shout-out and say, "Hey! Teachers! Which of your students are gifted?" you're likely to get data that are neither useful nor valid. However, if you put together a carefully prepared set of characteristics that the gifted child will need to be successful in the program options you offer, teachers are more likely to pick accurately. The same is true for parents and peers.

So why do teachers, especially, get a bad rap when it comes to their competency in identifying gifted students? It all stems from a small study done by Pegnato and Birch in 1959 that concluded that "teachers do not locate gifted children effectively or efficiently enough to place much relevance on them for screening (gifted children)" (p. 303). For more than four decades, this study gained almost mystical credibility as to the flawed practice of teacher identification. Then, Gagné came along in 1994 and reanalyzed the data, separating the "efficiency" of this process from its "effectiveness." His conclusion? "[T]eachers do not come out worse than most other sources of information" (p. 126). Now, that's not a ringing endorsement, by any means, but his conclusion has stood the test of time: If done well, teacher input can be a valuable tool in our identification arsenal. So can parent identification. So can peer identification.

Earlier, I mentioned that Annemarie Roeper had developed a method of assessment for young gifted children that focused on "measuring" what Roeper called their "inner worlds." This approach, The Annemarie Roeper Method of Qualitative Assessment (QA), has been in use for more than 20 years and still, even after Roeper's death in 2012, continues to be employed by practitioners she had trained.

Here is some background that led Roeper to develop QA. After Annemarie and her husband George transformed their Michigan-based school into a school for the gifted in 1956, they would often interview the young applicants and, on the basis of these interviews, estimate the child's IQ. Over many years and many children, the Roepers found that "we were surprised when our independent assessment almost always coincided with the results of the IQ test . . . it became more clear that the IQ test gave us only a partial answer" (Roeper, n.d., p. 1).

When Roeper retired from her school in 1980, she began to develop her QA methodology more systematically, based on her belief that "the human psyche is one of enormous complexity, not fully measurable by standardized psychometric examinations . . . the only instrument complex enough to understand a human being is another human being" (Roeper, 2007, p. 3). By combining her knowledge of gifted characteristics, as well as her finely tuned skills of empathy and intuition, Roeper created a procedure that involved an opening interview with parents, and an extended visit (90 minutes or so) with the child. The only agenda for the time spent with the child was to "discover who you are." Thus, Roeper and the child would play games, talk, read, or do any other activities that were initiated by the young boy or girl. When the child's "counter evaluation" of Roeper concluded and mutual trust was established ("the child's eyes are the most important clue"; Roeper, 2004, p. 33) genuine aspects of the child's self would emerge.

At the conclusion of the visit, Roeper would meet again with the parents and provide a written follow-up shortly thereafter. Roeper (2007) concluded that,

> we have learned that through the QA Method we can recognize the degree of giftedness, and the qualities that are attached to this, and knowing this will help us in trying to find the best environment in which this soul may thrive. (p. 13)

The QA Method is now being used by a second generation of practitioners who themselves were trained by Roeper. In the realm of identification practices that consider the entirety of the gifted child's life, the QA Method is the most complete and elegant of the bunch.

So, as you begin to examine the ins-and-outs of gifted student identification, remember this: A precise judgment of a child's abilities by someone who knows him or her well is more valuable than an imprecise number that neither knows nor cares about the kid who took the test.

Tenet #3: Tweaking the WISC-IV. In introducing this section on identification, I mentioned that I would not provide a laundry list of tests and other assessment instruments to use for gifted child identification. I'll stick with that statement—with this one exception of mentioning the Wechsler Intelligence Scale for Children (WISC). Of all the individually administered IQ tests available, the WISC is the most widely used. However, if psychologists are not familiar with the characteristics of gifted children and/or have seldom tested potentially gifted kids using the WISC, children with extreme intelligence might come out with a lower, less accurate IQ score. Happily, there are ways around this hurdle, as reviewed below.

First, a bit of "WISC-tory." The test first appeared in 1949, developed by David Wechsler. It's intent then, as now, was to provide an IQ score for children from ages 6–16 (there are other Wechsler tests for younger children and adults). Over the decades, different versions of the test appeared as new norms were developed and test items added or eliminated to be more representative of the current population of kids being tested. The latest version, the WISC-IV, or fourth edition, was released in 2003 and is available in both English and Spanish versions. The biggest change in the WISC-IV is the elimination of the two scores that, in earlier editions, were used to compute the IQ: the "verbal" and "performance" scores. In their place, the WISC-IV now contains 10 required subtests that yield both a "Full Scale" IQ and several other scores in the following areas: verbal, comprehension, perceptual reasoning, working memory, and processing speed. Although an IQ score of 160 is possible (the average IQ is 100, by the way), very few gifted children score above 140 on the WISC-IV (Silverman, Gilman, & Falk, n.d.).

But there was trouble in testing paradise: Psychologists who worked with gifted kids noted how some gifted children's scores were being depressed by the WISC-IV; thus, they began to advocate that changes in the administration of the test be made. Subsequently, the National Association for Gifted Children issued an official Position Statement in 2008 detailing how a General Ability Index (GAI) can be determined by using just six of the WISC-IV's subtests. This did two things: It eliminated several subtests that tended to lower the scores of gifted children (including working memory and processing speed), and it cut down on the time and cost of administering the test, without compromising the validity of the test results. Soon thereafter, the publisher of the WISC-IV, Pearson Assessments, issued a technical report that urged psychologists to follow the NAGC recommendations when assessing children for giftedness (Raiford, Weiss, Rolfhus, & Coalson, 2008).

Pearson Assessments then released a second technical report that offers "extended norms" as a supplement to the Full Scale score (Zhu, Cayton, Weiss, & Gabel, 2008). This allowed for test items that the child had gotten correct but were not previously counted in the scoring to be used in determining the Full Scale score. This extension allowed for the possibility of children scoring as high as 210 as a GAI or Full Scale score—a marked improvement for gifted children whose scores, heretofore, were measured at a lower than accurate level.

As the NAGC (2008) Position Statement concluded, if the extended norms guidelines are followed, "the WISC-IV offers an effective reasoning test with a good balance between verbally administered abstract reasoning and language items and tasks that assess visual-spatial and non-verbal reasoning" (p. 2).

Why should you care, as an educator or parent, about the intricacies of test design? Because if a potentially gifted child is being assessed by someone who is not aware of the presence and importance of these technical reports, the WISC-IV results will not be as valid an indicator of the child's true abilities as they could be. But armed with such knowledge, a parent or educator of gifted kids can speak with the psychologist with authority prior to test administration. The end result—a more accurate test score—will benefit everyone.

Certainly, every test that a child takes, from a spelling quiz on Friday morning, to the achievement tests given en masse each year, to a one-on-one IQ test, is going to favor some children over others. So scrutiny is not a bad thing, especially if a child's access to school programs is dependent on a particular score. Asking questions about the assessments whose results you must live with, as an educator or a parent, is doing your due diligence on behalf of the kids in your care.

Tenet #4: As soon as you think you're done, you're not. As mentioned earlier, gifted identification is a process, not a one-shot event. Of course, for the sake of efficiency, there may be a window of time during the school year when a general search for gifted children occurs. This is often in the spring, as test data are more generally available by then and, if teachers are to be used in the identification process, they'll have had the children being considered for identification for a better part of an academic year, optimizing the likelihood of accurate observations. So there is nothing wrong with having a scheduled time for gifted identification to take place—just know that some gifted children will make themselves known outside of this identification window.

Take the case of Chip, a former student of mine I highlighted in an earlier publication (Delisle & Lewis, 2003):

Chip, a fourth grader, had never been considered gifted by any teacher or by virtue of his test scores. In fact, his only special placement was in the school's learning disabilities program, where he went daily for individual help in writing and reading. But the new reading specialist was amazed at Chip's advanced vocabulary and command of abstract concepts, especially about politics. He discussed Chip's knowledge base with the boy's mother, suggesting that Chip might be considered for gifted services. Chip's mother nodded in both agreement and surprise. "We've always known he was smart," she explained, "but we never figured anyone at school would see a kid with learning disabilities as gifted, too." (p. 34)

Kids like Chip, who have a coexisting disability, are frequently missing from the candidate pool when it comes to gifted identification. So are kids who move in from another town, state, or country midyear that neither identified nor served gifted kids. So are kids who fly under the gifted radar due to other factors: being troublemakers or class clowns, quiet kids who perform poorly on standardized assessments, students of poverty whose high abilities might involve nonacademic tasks, or those who hide their giftedness for fear of isolating their classmates who think being smart is not cool.

A good way to ensure that kids like these outliers are not missed in the gifted identification process is to compile a list of student names of candidates who *do* qualify for gifted services. Then, distribute this list to teachers and ask, "Is there a student of yours (past or present) whose name is *not* on this list who you believe needs a closer look?" Although not a failsafe measure, this process proves its worth if you get even a few mentions of students to reconsider, especially if a particular student is named by multiple teachers. (Be warned, though: When the list of identified student names is distributed to teachers, you'll likely hear an occasional "How can *that* kid be gifted?" indicating that the teacher making this statement likely has a stereotypic view of giftedness that equates with high achievement and good classroom behavior. Don't look for a teacher like this to be a good spotter of "hidden giftedness" in children.) Once the names of these outliers are compiled, that's the time to probe deeper: interview the child, scour school records to find any hints of high ability through previous test scores or teacher comments, and observe the child in the setting that caused the nominating teacher to see a spark of brilliance. And if the picture still remains cloudy after all of these assessments and observations, then that's when it's time to bring in the heavy artillery: a school psychologist who can conduct a one-on-one comprehensive assessment, including an individual IQ test, to determine a student's obvious and hidden strengths. Expensive? Perhaps, but less costly than losing a gifted life to mediocrity.

In sum, even with procedures like these, it's still possible to miss some children who could benefit from a gifted identification and the services that accompany it—hey, we're human, we make mistakes, and our insights are sometimes shallow. Still, by keeping an open mind and an open door, and by using all of the quantitative and qualitative measures at our disposal, it is likely that the vast majority of children who should get identified as gifted . . . will be.

IMPLEMENTING INNOVATIVE AND COMPREHENSIVE PROGRAMMING PRACTICES

In the introduction to their book, *Exam Schools*, which investigates 165 highly selective public high schools among the 22,568 high schools in America, Finn and Hockett (2012) posed the following questions:

1. Is the United States providing *all* of its young people the education that they need in order to make the most of their capacities?
2. Have we neglected to raise the ceiling while we've struggled to lift the floor? As the country strives to toughen its academic standards, close its wide achievement gaps . . . and "leave no child behind," is it also challenging its high-

achieving and highly-motivated students—and those who may not yet be high achievers but can learn substantially more than the minimum?

3. Is America making wise investments in its own future prosperity and security by ensuring that its high-potential children are well-prepared to break new ground and assume leadership roles? (pp. 1–2)

Questions such as these elevate the education of gifted children into the realms of economics and national security, a far cry away from the suburban second-grade classroom awash in glitter paint and alphabet placards. Indeed, serious stuff requiring an introspective look at the ways we do—or don't—educate our nation's most capable children.

In this section, I'll suggest some places we might go if we wish to offer a comprehensive set of services to gifted children, from preschool through college. Some of the ideas are embedded in fields peripheral to gifted education, while others come directly from expert practitioners who live in the world of gifted kids every day. The aim here is to consider what types of educational *provisions* are necessary to make up a complete gifted *program*. A provision alone—say, an elementary gifted program that meets one day a week or a secondary school that allows students to earn high school and college credits simultaneously—is insufficient unless coupled with other options that take the totality of a gifted child's education into consideration.

THE 7 C'S: BUILDING UPON A FIRM FOUNDATION

Before asking *what* should be done in schools to benefit gifted children—or any learner, for that matter—people in charge need to consider the guiding principles that steer their curriculum and instruction. Ronald Ferguson (2010), from Harvard University's Center for Teacher Effectiveness, offered up his "7 C's," which were compiled after surveying students in thousands of classrooms about what teacher behaviors are most effective in helping them to learn:

◇ *Care*: Teachers help students feel emotionally safe and go out of their way to help.

◇ *Control*: Teachers are able to maintain order and keep the classroom calm and students on-task.

◇ *Clarify*: Teachers are able to diagnose students' skills and knowledge, and then are able to explain ideas in multiple ways.

◇ *Challenge*: Teachers press students to reason their way through challenging questions and confront students if their effort is unsatisfactory.

◇ *Captivate*: Teachers make the material interesting and relevant to what students care about.

◇ *Confer*: Teachers ask students for their views and provide positive reinforcement for their efforts. Teachers also encourage students to express themselves to one another.

◇ *Consolidate*: Teachers help students organize material and help them remember and reason. They help with reviewing and summarizing skills by showing students how to find relationships between ideas and identify patterns.

Certainly, students bear some of the responsibility for their own learning, and if their teachers exhibit the behaviors and attitudes highlighted above, then the provisions that follow will be that much more likely to succeed.

DESIGNING EDUCATIONAL SERVICES FOR GIFTED CHILDREN, PRESCHOOL–ELEMENTARY GRADES

Why not start with the best?: the gifted services provided by the Paradise Valley Unified School District (PVUSD) in Phoenix, AZ (see http://www.pvschools.net/gifted). The PVUSD is a racially and culturally diverse district of 33,000 students. With school options that include everything from digital learning experiences to a K–12 International Baccalaureate program, the PVUSD also offers a comprehensive selection of services for gifted children, starting in preschool. With both half-day and full-day options, the gifted preschool program employs teachers who are certified as both early

I am the mother of a gifted Black female. I suspect she also has a specific learning disability in spelling. She excels in school and on achievement tests, but scores average on intelligence tests. School personnel—teachers and psychologists—are perplexed, unsure of how to identify and serve her. Her gifts and talents are being denied, with too much attention on her perceived deficits. Scholarship exists on twice-exceptional gifted students, but it fails to address culturally specific issues of Black students who have gifted and other special needs. We must address cultural needs in both gifted and special education to save students like my daughter.

Michelle Trotman Scott, Associate Professor,
University of West Georgia, Carrollton, GA

childhood educators and gifted child specialists. With a maximum of 20 students per class, the preschool curriculum offers instruction in critical and creative thinking and has accelerated content meshed with integrative technology. Once students "graduate" from the gifted preschool, they can stay at the same school and participate in self-contained gifted classes until the end of their sixth-grade year.

For students whose giftedness may not require such extensive services, various other provisions are also in place:

◇ "cluster grouping" of gifted children in elementary classrooms, so that at least several identified gifted students are together in their elementary years;

◇ honors level classes in grades 4–6;

◇ a "uniquely gifted" program, grades 1–6, for children who are twice exceptional;

◇ a "nonverbal honors core" for gifted students from culturally or linguistically diverse backgrounds; and

◇ a "digital learning experience," which provides an afterschool/weekend supplement to students attending local private or charter schools, as well as PVUSD and other school districts.

What makes PVUSD stand out is both the breadth and depth of its offerings for young gifted children. Taking a tiered approach, gifted kids of all persuasions—highly gifted, moderately gifted, gifted with disabilities, etc.—find a place to fit within the PVUSD schools. These programs are enhanced by professional development opportunities for staff and community presentations for parents of gifted kids or those just interested in learning more. If you are looking for a "complete package" of how to serve gifted young children, PVUSD is the Holy Grail you seek.

But what if a school district is not able to offer this array of services? Perhaps it is too small to provide such extensive options, or maybe a lack of emphasis on serving gifted children in past years means that the PVUSD model is one to strive for, yet one that will take years to build up to. Let's consider what is realistic in such cases using a template provided by Johnsen (2011) that asks those interested in serving gifted children to consider six elements of effective gifted program development:

1. *Learning and development*: What preliminary work must be done to ensure that educators recognize the unique learning and growth needs of gifted students?

2. *Assessment*: Are the instruments used to assess giftedness valid and varied, using both qualitative and quantitative measures? What steps are taken to assess gifted students' learning on a regular basis?

3. *Curriculum planning and instruction*: How are advanced and enriched curricula selected, adapted, and created, making certain that creative and critical thinking skills are addressed?

4. *Learning environments*: Do the various learning environments in which gifted children are placed provide intellectual safety, trust, and self-exploration, allowing students to explore their own unique aspects?

5. *Programming*: Is there a continuum of services, properly funded, across grade levels that addresses cognitive, affective, and academic elements of a gifted child's life?

6. *Professional development*: Are staff development options regarding the educational and emotional lives of gifted children available to *all* educators, not just those responsible for gifted program management?

These ideas are all well and good, but how might they translate into specific program options? Let's use the Olympic Games as the model for planning gifted program services for young gifted children, awarding three levels of medals: bronze, silver, and gold.

At the **bronze** level, the gifted program options are minimal and scattered. Likely, only one person in the district is responsible for everything from gifted identification to teaching gifted children to managing administrative duties. Children are seldom identified prior to second grade, and the single most visible program option is a one-day-per-week pull-out program that the gifted children attend. Classroom teachers and principals are invested only minimally in the gifted services, feeling that if the gifted kids get together one day a week, that their needs are being met sufficiently. There is little coordination between what happens in the gifted program and what occurs in the regular classroom, and time constraints on the gifted teacher/coordinator are such that regular communication with teachers who have identified gifted children in their classrooms is limited. Gifted children may or may not be clustered in just a few classrooms, depending on the whim of the principal, who may either believe that the clustering is sensible and efficient, or conversely, thinks that it is only "fair" if every classroom teacher has a gifted student or two in his or her classroom.

You might be wondering why such a programmatically challenged set of options deserves even a bronze medal. The reality is, school districts must begin somewhere, and the addition of even a single teacher who is responsible for gifted program management is a step in the right direction. With a lot of hard work and stamina, such program options might lead to the next level: the silver medal.

At the **silver** medal level, gifted program responsibilities are split: one person serves as the program administrator while one or more gifted teachers are responsible for day-to-day instruction. Identification begins in first grade, unless a kindergarten student is so exceptional that his or her needs must be addressed through some form of acceleration. Cluster grouping of gifted students is consistent across district elementary schools, and the gifted coordinator plays a role with the principals in gifted student placement decisions. Also, an acceleration policy is in place and has Board of Education approval, ensuring that acceleration decisions align across the various schools. The gifted teachers work on a regular basis with the identified students in a pull-out setting, but also work with classroom teachers in designing whole-class instruction or learning centers that focus on creative or critical thinking skills. Staff development offerings include information on understanding and teaching gifted students, and "cluster teachers" are required to have such professional development sessions. There is at least one meeting annually for parents of identified gifted children to hear from a speaker on some aspect of giftedness.

Obviously, there is more "buy-in" by principals and classroom teachers in this silver medal example—and that is a huge plus. In the bronze medal scenario, the gifted program is isolated and apart from most day-to-day school operations, meaning that it is a likely target for elimination when budgets get tight. However, when the gifted program meshes well with other elements of the school, as in the silver medal scenario, it is likely to be seen, over time, as an integral part of school operation, making it a less likely target for the budget ax.

Of course, the epitome of excellence is the **gold** medal and, in a gifted program, it might look something like this: The gifted program administrator is a full member of the district's administrative team, meaning that at every meeting of upper level district personnel, there is a voice in the room advocating for gifted kids. A Board of Education-adopted "Mission Statement" for gifted education exists, meshing its goals with those of the district's overall vision. Identification is available from kindergarten, and teachers are a part of the identification committee that screens potential candidates for the gifted program, with particular attention paid to gifted children who may have a disability or other special need. Instructionally speaking, multiple teachers are employed full- or part-time to serve gifted students exclusively, although the gifted teachers continue to stay connected to their classroom counterparts through common times for planning and lesson preparation. Cluster grouping of gifted students is a well-established and accepted practice. A well-designed curriculum for gifted students exists, ensuring continuity from one grade level (and teacher) to the next. The gifted coordinator meets regularly with the gifted program staff and, 1 or 2 days each month, meets with gifted students in an informal "lunch bunch" setting to keep a finger on the pulse of the program's success from the students' points of view. An appealing and informative website exists and is updated regularly with lesson plans and information on some aspect of gifted child development. Never a static program, the services offered may vary from year to year, depending on student need, which is the driver of all decisions made on behalf of the district's gifted population. In fact, discussions are ongoing to initiate an International Baccalaureate program at the primary level that will mesh with the IB programs already in operation at the middle and high school levels.

Even a small school district can have a gold medal program, and conversely, a large and affluent school district might come up short. The most essential ingredient to excellence is the selection of the personnel who will manage and teach the gifted program, as their advocacy, knowledge, and empathy will make or break a program that, truth be told, is sometimes seen as more frivolous than essential by naysayers who haven't bought into the idea that gifted services are important.

DESIGNING EDUCATIONAL SERVICES FOR GIFTED CHILDREN, GRADES 6–12

Many times, school districts that offer identifiable gifted programs in the elementary years do not do so once middle school hits. There will be any array of honors courses at both the middle and high schools, but if most secondary teachers were asked if a gifted program existed beyond grade 6, their answer would be "no." And they would be both right . . . and wrong.

Let's return to Paradise Valley as an example of this right/wrong conundrum. In PVUSD, each middle school provides honors courses in the basic subjects: math, language arts, science, and social studies. In addition, two middle schools maintain an IB program and, just for good measure, an Honors Academy of Pre-Engineering and World Languages is available for interested and capable seventh and eighth graders. At the high school level, both honors and AP courses exist in abundance, as does the IB Diploma Programme. Further, a Digital Academy exists that offers a traditional high school experience with gifted courses taught in a project-based, technology-driven format. The Digital Academy's focus is on information technology, its subject matter is integrated across disciplines, and with dual credit options available, graduating seniors may have already completed 30+ hours of college coursework on top of their AP college credits.

Are these "gifted services"? It depends on your definition of such. Certainly, identified gifted students are enrolled in these options, but so are other high-achieving students who may never have been identified as gifted. Simultaneously, as the eligibility for access to these services increases, the stamina required to succeed in these options makes student participation more rigorous. More than any other criteria, including a gifted label, self-selection is the most important decider of "who takes what" at the secondary level—in PVUSD and virtually every other school district nationwide.

But gifted and other capable secondary-level students are more than mere academic behemoths and, if the many needs of these capable teens are to be fully channeled and challenged, then the middle and high school offerings need to provide both breadth and depth. That's where the "Inventory of Excellence" comes in, a checklist of sorts to determine whether the secondary schools with which you are most familiar rise to the gold medal level when it comes to serving gifted students.

The Inventory of Excellence. Sit down with the faculty and staff of any secondary school and ask them what options exist—academic and extracurricular—that benefit gifted students. You'll be amazed at the array of options that this inventory provides! Here are some likely candidates:

◇ honors-level classes in core subject areas, and AP courses in high school, with grades in these courses "weighted" so that a "B" in an honors-level class carries the weight of an "A" in a nonhonors course in the same subject;

◇ middle school students awarded high school credit for taking out-of-level courses (e.g., taking geometry in seventh or eighth grade) and high school students getting college credit for courses taken online or at a local university;

⬦ a variety of athletic, musical, technological, and fine arts options in the form of "clubs" or teams (e.g., forensics, robotics, or literary magazines);

⬦ local, state, and national competitions, such as Academic Decathlon, National History Day, and Science Olympiad;

⬦ an independent study option at the high school level that allows students to pursue personal areas of passion for course credit; and

⬦ the opportunity to do mentorships or internships in an area of possible career selection with local businesses, hospitals, and community agencies.

These options alone would do a secondary school proud, but the list doesn't have to stop there. Additional items that will get a middle or high school from good to great when it comes to serving its gifted students would also include these possibilities:

⬦ a monthly, field-trip based enrichment program for identified middle school gifted students. I directed a program like this in an Ohio school district. Project Plus ran for 10 years, and my students and I visited places such as a children's hospital, the Federal Reserve Bank of Cleveland, an Amish schoolhouse, a historical cemetery, a modern art museum, and the Honors College of a nearby university. With a budget of $0—I had only a school bus and a driver at my disposal—much learning occurred on these monthly excursions, proving that excellence in gifted programming doesn't need to cost a lot of money;

⬦ "school within a school" academies (similar to the pre-engineering academy at PVUSD) that focus on one or more fields of specialty in the arts, sciences, technology, or humanities;

⬦ magnet schools, not unlike the public high schools reviewed in the book *Exam Schools*, that attract (hence, the magnet) gifted students and provide serious, purposeful places where competition runs rampant in a supportive, engaging learning environment; and

◇ "Scholars Academies," which are high schools located on college campuses, where students take both high school and college courses beginning in ninth grade. Upon high school graduation, students also receive an associate's degree. Three such examples include: The Scholars Academy of Horry County, SC (http://www.scholars.horrycountyschools.net); Collegiate High School in Corpus Christi, TX (http://www.chs.ccisd.us); and the Illinois Math and Science Academy in Aurora, IL (http://www3.imsa.edu).

WHY SPECIAL SCHOOLS MAKE A DIFFERENCE

When students attend a school like the Scholars Academy in Conway, SC, the benefits do not end upon high school graduation. Here's proof:

◇ *"I graduated from New York University 2 years early, receiving a B.F.A. in drama, with honors, from the Tisch School of the Arts. Since graduating, I relocated to Los Angeles and booked my first co-star role on a television series. I have strong hopes that my career will continue to flourish. I could not have accomplished this without having graduated from Scholars Academy. Not only was I able to graduate from NYU in 2 years, but [did so] with a 3.7 GPA. the payoff of attending Scholars is far greater than I could ever have imagined. I am a living testament that intelligence is not a life sentence to being a doctor or lawyer."—Nikki King*

◇ *"I am a student at Agnes Scott College in Atlanta where I am studying neuroscience and public health. Currently, I am working with a professor researching Rett Syndrome, and I was recently published in the Behavioral Brain Research Journal. I am so thankful I attended Scholars Academy, because I probably wouldn't have had the opportunities I have now."—L. A. Ambrose*

The array of options open to secondary-level gifted students is limited only by the imagination. However, the most vital variable will never change: the expertise of their instructors and the teaching styles and attitudes they bring into their classrooms. Finn and Hockett (2012) pointed out that in the 165 "exam schools" they studied, the criterion cited most frequently by these schools when hiring teachers was "subject matter knowledge," mentioned by 92% of respondents as the most essential skill. The next most cited criterion?: "[A]bility to relate to, understand and/or engage adolescent learners," at 84%. According to one school administrator, "A program with high-achieving students needs faculty that can and will challenge students. However, teenagers are a unique entity and education needs to be age-appropriate and engaging" (Finn & Hockett, p. 51).

When gifted students (all students, really) are treated as the maturing young adults that they are by those responsible for their education, everyone gains.

So, in concluding this section, the question remains, "Is there *one best* program model or set of options that should be used in serving gifted students?" Until the day that every single gifted student has the exact same talents, personalities, strengths, and quirks, the answer to that question is "no." However, the road map laid out in this chapter should certainly provide some beneficial directions.

THIRTY YEARS LATER: WHAT HAPPENS WHEN GIFTED KIDS GROW UP?

The Study of Mathematically Precocious Youth (SMPY) began at Johns Hopkins University in 1971. Its goal was to find and educate profoundly gifted youth who scored in the top 1% on the Scholastic Aptitude Test (SAT) before the age of 13. These students would then enroll in college classes at a time when most of their contemporaries were entering eighth grade.

So what happens to kids like these when they become adults? Did they measure up to the high expectations that their aptitude indicated they had? A study (Kell, Lubinski, & Benbow, 2013) of 320 SMPY alumni who are now 38 years old indicates that for many, their promise was fulfilled. With occupations as varied as teachers, writers, physicians, artists, and engineers, these 320 are a very accomplished lot: 203 have at least a master's degree and 142 have doctorates. Collectively, they hold 49 patents and have produced 14 theater and 21 musical productions. They have received millions of dollars in grants from corporations and agencies such as GM, GE, NASA, Intel, and the CIA. Nine of the participants are presidents or vice-presidents of corporations or nonprofits (keep in mind, they are only 38 years old), and they have dozens of publications, including professional papers, poetry, a nonfiction book, and two novels. As the authors stated, "their leadership positions in business, health care, law, the professoriate and STEM . . . suggest that many are outstanding creators of modern culture, constituting a precious human-capital resource" (p. 648).

Would these prolific adults have performed as well had they not participated in SMPY? That's a question that is impossible to answer. However, why take the chance of letting identified talent lie fallow when, instead, it can be nurtured into such a wide array of human excellence and ingenuity by programs like SMPY?

STEM, STEMM, OR STEAM?: OTHER CURRICULAR CONSIDERATIONS FOR GIFTED STUDENTS

Because America seems to be most interested in spending money on education only when a crisis looms (remember Sputnik?), it's no surprise that STEM programs have become the newest rage, especially in middle and high schools. As discussed in a previous chapter, the acronym stands for science, technology, engineering, and mathematics, and it's hard to find a funded project anywhere in education that does not have at least some focus in these areas. According to an analysis made by the Federal Inventory of STEM Education Fast-Track Action Committee (2011), the federal government has been a huge supporter of STEM education, spending $3.4 billion in fiscal year 2010 for STEM-related projects. Virtually every tentacle of the federal government's long reach has contributed something, with the National Science Foundation (NSF) and the U.S. Department of Education (USDOE) making up the bulk of the expenditures that have funded nearly 250 projects nationwide. Smaller monetary contributions by the Department of Defense, the Environmental Protection Agency, and even the Department of Agriculture make up the rest of these expenditures. This $3.4 billion amounts to less than 1% of the $1.1 trillion spent annually on education across America, yet it is still a remarkable figure. And that is just *federal* dollars; states contribute huge additional sums on their own to STEM-related initiatives.

Higher education, industry, and philanthropy have contributed buckets more money, the most prominent of many projects being the U-Teach Institute (http://www.uteach-institute.org), which began at the University of Texas in 1996 and has since spread to 34 other universities in seven states. The goal of U-Teach is to train educators to become the next generation of public school STEM teachers, and it has received strong financial support from ExxonMobil (that makes sense) and the Michael and Susan Dell Foundation, which focuses on using education and social policy to aid children in poverty worldwide.

Why the rush to train STEM teachers? Well, according to the National Center for Education Statistics, in a study published in 2011 by Hill and Gruber, more than 30% of chemistry and physics teachers did not major in these subjects in college and do not have certification to teach these subjects. In addition, 25% of secondary-level math educators do not hold a math degree. This issue is most acute in middle school, where only 10% of physical science teachers have certification in that specific field. So if you have a middle school science teacher slogging through a curriculum that is foreign territory, how likely is it that students will look to science as something exciting enough to pursue in high school—and beyond?

The anticipation is that if intelligent people can be convinced to become STEM teachers, their middle and high school students will want to grow up to become an engineer or mathematician because they are so excited about the career opportunities that await them. And I hope that is true; sincerely I do.

But then I read a comment like this one from an 11th-grade girl:

> . . . what about medicine? It should be STEMM, and yes, this is central to my future. I am going to become a radiologist. I have always wanted to be in the health professions and my aspirations are to be the best of the best. (Schultz, 2012, p. 9)

This girl has a point, as a recent analysis (Lakhan & Laird, 2009) of the dire need for physicians, especially primary care physicians, predicts a deficit of more than 200,000 primary care physicians by the year 2025, especially in rural areas and communities of high poverty. Who knows? Perhaps by adding a new "M" to the STEM acronym, the possibilities for us as a nation and for the individuals who inhabit America broadens even more.

And then there is this observation from a college freshman:

> There is too much focus on STEM. Everyone is heading in that direction, and from what I've seen, engineering specifically is at a point of overabundance of trained professionals who don't have jobs or have low paying jobs. I believe there is going to be a glut of STEM-focused graduates in the coming years. Nobody seems to think about this, though. I've altered my career path to be cross-trained and flexible. I believe having strong and creative thinking skills is much more important than content training. (Schultz, 2012, p. 9)

How right she is, as Koebler (2011) reported that the majority of the jobs that STEM-related programs create will not need an advanced degree, but one that can be received at a technical school or community college. Employers will be looking for more skilled-based operators rather than multiple-degreed thinkers.

So are we creating one problem while solving another? Time will tell whether these STEM initiatives pay off in ways that justify their huge expense.

Of course, the additional dollars spent on STEM have to be found somewhere—and sadly, that somewhere over the past decade often has been arts-related education. In a study of 1,200 public schools commissioned by the U.S. Department of Education (Parsad & Spiegelman-Westat, 2012), it was found that between the years 2000 and 2009, millions of children were no longer getting instruction in the arts. The report cited that 1.3 million elementary students nationwide are getting no music instruction in school; the figure for secondary schools is 800,000 students. Four million elementary students get no instruction in visual arts, a figure especially true in schools of high poverty. Anecdotally, in 2011, the Broward County, FL, schools reduced arts education funding by one third in its middle and high schools. And in the New York City Public Schools, funding for arts education was reduced by 68% between 2006–2007.

The sad irony of this is that when arts education began in America's public schools in the 19th century, it was done to enhance cognitive skills of students. Specifically, music instruction began to help newly arrived immigrants learn English and to lessen their accents through singing, while visual arts instruction began because of the link that was noted between being able to draw and being able to design machines that were a vital cog in the Industrial Revolution. And today? More often than not, when public school budgets need to be cut, such a "frill" as arts education joins gifted education programs as often among the first to go.

Bob Schultz (2012), the compiler of the two student excerpts that grace this section on STEM, made this astute observation:

> The Humanities teach us all how to interact with others; how to see our lives through the eyes and viewpoints of others. Philosophy allows us to grapple with big ideas and the realization that some questions just don't have answers that are permanent. Theatre

and visual and performing arts teach us how to communicate and express ourselves effectively.

We need more than science, technology, engineering, mathematics, or medicine. We need individuals who are thinkers, tinkerers, and dreamers. We need a focus on STEAMM. (p. 9)

At this juncture, perhaps it's worth reiterating a quote from John Gardner that is found earlier in this book: "the society that scorns excellence in plumbing as a humble activity and tolerates shoddiness in philosophy because it is an exalted activity will have neither good pipes nor good philosophy: neither our pipes nor our theories will hold water."

It's time to put STEM into its proper perspective as one of many possibilities for our nation's continued growth. There are too many ways that individuals can contribute to our world to laud one area of emphasis over another.

21ST-CENTURY LEARNING

I often wonder if many of our students feel like they are time traveling as they walk through the school door each morning. As they cross the threshold, do they feel as if they are entering a simulation of life in the 1980's? Then, at the end of the school day, do they feel that they have returned to the 21st century? (H. H. Jacobs, 2010, p. 1)

This quote, from curriculum specialist Heidi Hayes Jacobs, speaks volumes as to the disconnect between how today's K–12 students are taught by their "digital immigrant" teachers—those of us who still remember overhead projectors as high-tech—and the lives that students experience as "digital natives" once the school dismissal bell rings. There are many adjectives that could be used to describe America's schools but, as Milton Chen (2010) has noted, "*edgy* wouldn't be one of them" (p. 4). Yet even though today's students never existed in a world *without* iPods, laptops, the Internet, and ebooks, they are *still* using voluminous school textbooks, the contents of which are often obsolete even before they are published. This disconnect between what students access on their own and what they are provided with at school is a divide that cannot be ignored. And, as Chen noted, this is not an issue relevant only to isolated portions of our country or schools that lack even the basic essentials to help students—it is even true in Silicon Valley:

> Within an hour's drive of the campuses of Google, Apple, Intel, Cisco and many other companies that brought us the world of digital information we now inhabit, you would be hard-pressed to find a single school in which every student and teacher has 24/7 access to the tools that these companies have created. (Chen, 2010, p. 5)

In order to bridge this increasingly large gap between what students bring into our schools and what we offer them in return, the shift in our nation's thinking needs to be seismic, not sporadic. This issue is especially acute for gifted students who, even if enrolled in gifted programs or highly academic courses, are still taught in a structure where "learning" math begins 46 minutes after you have finished "learning" social studies. The natural bonds that exist between and among academic disciplines is stifled by a bell-driven, test-oriented school culture that refuses to budge from its 19th-century roots.

Except in some schools, where 21st-century skills were being taught even before Al Gore invented the Internet. Case in point: A company's board meeting is concluding after its members discussed all points relevant to money/finance, advertising, and display. Money/finance confidently predicted record sales, advertising presented a proposal to reach beyond printed materials into social media outlets, and the display team provided several options for showcasing the company's newest products. Spirits were high and, at the board meeting's end, people cheered, clapped, and sang. The singing was not to pat themselves on the back for great sales, but rather, to celebrate the birthdays of several of its members—a few of them were turning 9 years old that week.

This scenario was presented by J. J. Morrow, Lower School Director at Michigan's Roeper School for the Gifted, as he documented how a classroom full of youngsters was reviewing the status of their "Recycle Store," an annual venture into creating art objects from recyclable materials like aluminum cans, glass jars, and cardboard, with all profits going to a local organization of the students' collective choice. Intended originally as a project to bolster math skills and concepts, this store project also brings in, naturally, other core skills in reading and writing. Further, those so-called 21st-century skills that have been a part of learning since time began—critical thinking, creativity, collaboration, and communication—are in evidence daily in this activity.

The Recycle Store is not an exception at the Roeper School— it is the rule. Unburdened by many of the "have-to's" that public schools must endure in the name of accountability, the Roeper School expects that, left to their own devices, gifted students will learn what is important to them with the help of teachers who will guide their journeys.

But why can't public schools have such freedoms? Why do state accountability rules continue to stress low-level skills and knowledge that, in isolation, have little real application? If two of the end results of education are lifelong learning and the pursuit of individual goals, doesn't an operation like the Recycle Store make sense? If a high school senior wishes to do a year-long internship that puts to practical use the skills and concepts she has learned in the previous 11 years of schooling instead of taking unneeded electives to fill her school day, shouldn't she be encouraged to do so? If it makes sense to group kids of multiple ages in the same classrooms based on their levels of readiness to learn, who's to fault such a sensible notion?

Sadly, the naysayers are the same people who often bemoan the state of our nation's education system; individuals and institutions without the political will to move beyond the familiar into the realm of the possible, and blockers who insist that without the onus of standardized testing hanging over their heads, educators will slack off and students' educations will be in jeopardy. If such extraordinary learning can happen so successfully at the Roeper School . . . it can happen elsewhere as well. What's missing? The guts to try it and the trust required in teachers and learners that does not exist today in the toxic atmosphere that is public education.

Call the Recycle Store "personalized learning," a new buzz term that is being bandied about in the same breath as 21st-century skills. But once again, at the Roeper School, personalized learning is not an innovation, but merely a necessary component of every child's education that has always been in fashion. Ask yourself these questions—the same ones that Roeper students are asked to consider at each stage in their learning:

◇ Who am I apart from the person I am when I am fulfilling others' expectations of me?

◇ Are there qualities I can discover, embrace, and celebrate in myself that cannot be measured?

◇ What are the opportunities for creating my own expectations, for pursuing my passions, and for creating personal criteria for judging the worthiness of my pursuits?

◇ Do I have time to pursue something for its own sake because it may be valuable, necessary, or enjoyable, not just a means to an end? (Seward, 2004, p. 12–13)

Most of us do not ask the question of "What is the greater good that comes from my educational endeavors?" yet there is no more essential question to answer. As author and educator Haim Ginnott (1972), observed, "reading, writing and arithmetic are important only if they serve to make our children more humane" (p. 317). If our gifted children are to thrive once they leave our care as young adults, then we must look beyond the educational programs that we offer them on paper; we must ask what skills they will need to be fully functioning, compassionate human beings. Using the Roeper School model as a springboard for shaking up the public school establishment is a fine place to begin.

THREE EXTRAORDINARY (AND FREE) OPPORTUNITIES

It's not often that "free" and "extraordinary" are used in the same sentence, as things that are well worth our efforts to explore usually cost at least something. Not in these three cases: the Khan Academy, TED Talks, and the Young Ambassador Program. Each of these innovations continues to change the educations and lives of gifted young people every day. Let's start with the newest of the three, the Khan Academy,

A graduate of MIT, Salman Khan was a young hedge fund manager who was tutoring his two cousins in math. Problem was, Khan was in Boston and his cousins lived in New Orleans. To save time (theirs and his), Khan decided to make a video of some lessons, posting them on YouTube. Next, a few things happened: Khan's cousins informed him that they liked him better as a tutor on YouTube than on the phone, as they could access him when they had time and could get him to repeat a concept they had trouble with by simply restarting the video. Then, Khan's videos started getting comments from others who watched them, praising both his instructional style and the videos' content. At some point, a star was born, as Khan quit his lucrative day job and began his not-for-profit Khan Academy. Currently, there are more than 3,000 videos available (http://www.khanacademy.org) on topics that range from mathematics to art history. What started as a one-man operation, with Khan's voiceover on each of the videos, is now voluminous, with guest instructors presenting videos in their particular areas of expertise. Every month, more than 1 million people access the videos, with more than 100,000 videos viewed each day,

As the availability of the videos has grown, so has the complexity of the Khan Academy's operation. For example, those who sign up with a Facebook or Google account (both are optional) gain access to "coaches" who can answer questions in a chat room format. Or users who wish to do so can partner with a "study buddy." Also, with so many topics now available, the lessons presented are tiered in terms of their complexity, creating a matrix of "knowledge maps" that take you, for instance, from simple addition all the way through calculus . . . and beyond. Assessment is done every step of the way, with the main

166

format being that you stick with one concept until you get 10 answers correct in a row. At that time, you move on to the logical next step.

In reviewing the Khan Academy, Barbara Branch (2012) declared that it "opens a revolutionary discussion of the approach to teaching and learning . . . it should be used as a resource and supplement for a curriculum that also includes problem solving and concept development" (p. 39). Branch further described the many ways that the Khan Academy videos can be useful:

1. *Compacting curriculum*: because each video is self-paced, students progress to more complex tasks as soon as they master easier ones;

2. *Flipped classrooms*: students are assigned videos as homework and practice what they learned from them the next day in their classrooms—the opposite of how instruction/homework usually works; hence, the "flipping";

3. *Homeschooling instruction*: with practice and assessments available for each lesson, the videos become a valuable addition to the homeschooler's toolbox; and

4. *Building motivation*: "the Khan Academy videos can provide a way for gifted students to review and practice a new learning without fear of others knowing that they have failed." (p. 40)

In addition to these benefits, there are more: Each video can be accessed in multiple languages, and subtitled captions can be applied for those viewers who are deaf. Students in rural areas with little access to specialized topics now have the world of Khan at their disposal, as evidenced by the state of Idaho receiving a private foundation grant in 2013 of $1.5 million to bring math, science, and history courses to 47 school districts—the first state in the nation to adopt such a plan (Dvorak, 2013). And in 2014, the College Board enlisted Khan Academy to provide free online preparation for the redesigned SAT exam. Lastly, according to reports that Khan has received from parents of children with autism, these youngsters find this form of learning very much in sync with their individual needs.

Indeed, the Khan Academy is one of the most useful online education tools aligned with the interests of many a gifted digital native.

A close cousin to the Khan Academy in terms of merit, if not content, is the popular and impressive array of videos available at TED Talks (http://www.TED.com). TED stands for Technology, Entertainment, and Design, a trio of innovations that TED founder, Richard Saul Wurman, saw converging in 1984. He sponsored an invitation-only conference that included a demonstration of how a Sony compact disc, combined with newly invented 3D graphics from Lucasfilm, could help in showing how to map coastlines with fractals newly discovered by mathematician Benoit Mandelbrot. Hmmm . . . perhaps not the most compelling debut in terms of audience appeal; in fact, the conference lost money and TED was put on the shelf for 6 years. When it reemerged under a new format, the invitation-only conference was held annually in Monterey, CA (it still is), and was designed for people who were "united by curiosity, open-mindedness and the desire to think outside the box" (TED, n.d., para. 2). Speakers have included such famous innovators as Herbie Hancock, Jane Goodall, Bill Gates, Bono, Billy Graham, Annie Lennox, Jane Fonda, and Al Gore, as well as hundreds of others of lesser fame but equally extraordinary accomplishment.

Purchased by the Sapling Foundation in 2001, TED continued to broaden its focus and to offer even more of what they do best—this time, in the form of TED Talks: free, downloadable videos that last anywhere from 6–20 minutes in duration. There are now more than 1,000 TED Talks available, including these that may be of particular interest to gifted children and teens:

◇ Aimee Mullins: a Paralympics competitor who tried out her artificial legs on stage;

◇ Thomas Suarez: a 12-year-old self-taught iPhone app developer;

◇ Lauren Hodge: a 14-year-old winner of the 2011 Google Science Fair contest for her study of the formation of carcinogens in different cooking methods for preparing chicken;

◇ the Sleepy Man Banjo Boys, a trio of brothers—ages 10, 14, and 15—who play amazing bluegrass music; and

◇ Jennifer Lin, a 14-year-old composer and pianist whose 6-minute improvisation brought her audience to tears.

TED now sponsors an annual TED Global Conference, in a different nation each year, as well as a TED Prize where the winner gets "one wish to change the world." The 2013 winner, educational researcher Sugata Mitra, received $1 million to build a "School in the Cloud"—a learning laboratory in India where children will embark on intellectual adventures by engaging and connecting with information and through online tutoring.

TED is designed to promote what many schools do not: innovation, open-endedness, curiosity, beauty, and fun. There is no way anyone could watch a sampling of TED Talks and not feel better about the status of our world and the people who inhabit it. Perhaps this is the greatest reason of all to introduce TED to gifted children and teens.

One of the most common stereotypes about gifted children is that they are all social outcasts and bookworms. In reality, most are like anyone else—friendly, funny, often silly, and compassionate. Investing in service-oriented gifted programming that takes young people out of the classroom to "give something back" to others would do much to change this commonly held misperception. These experiences also provide a venue for gifted students to develop executive functioning skills to match their intellects. Finally, and not to be underestimated, are the potentially enormous benefits to the communities where these young people live and learn. Put simply, it's a win-win-win situation.

Erik Schwinger, Former Program Coordinator,
Davidson Institute for Talent Development, Reno, NV

Just as the TED Prize helps to make one person's dream come true to change the world, the Young Ambassadors Program (YAP), sponsored by the Davidson Institute, does the same on a smaller scale.

Begun by Jan Davidson as an adjunct to the Young Scholars component of the Davidson Institute, the YAP's purpose is to foster learning and civic engagement in gifted young people through community service, volunteerism, and leadership. Students apply with a seed of an idea they wish to pursue and, if accepted, are guided along the way by online mentors and coaches. Over the course of a year, there are eight one-week, online seminars on topics such as writing a strategic plan, self-advocacy, fundraising, leadership, and public/media relations. In addition, each participant receives personalized support and guidance from a program advisor who helps the Young Ambassadors flesh out and implement their ideas. Covering any topic that has a service-related component, the YAP has financed, both monetarily and emotionally, projects like these, as reported by Schwinger and Delisle (2012):

◇ *Music to My Ears*: Ethan was not happy to see his school's music programs lost to budget cuts, so he began an all-volunteer team of middle and high school students who provide music lessons to elementary children. So far, his 18 volunteers have assisted more than 80 children (http://www.musictomyearshanover.org).

◇ *Community Recycling Program for a Better Tomorrow*: Thirteen-year-old Sachin grew concerned when he saw neighbors tossing away computers and electronics with their trash. Well aware of the dangers of e-waste, Sachin founded a nonprofit organization that has recycled and refurbished countless electronic items, raising thousands of dollars for UNICEF and the Hemophilia Foundation in the process (http://www.crcfbt.org).

◇ *A Hole in My Heart*: When 13-year-old Elizabeth's dog, Bubba, passed away, she felt a huge loss. Working diligently to research the grieving process, Elizabeth decided to produce a video that would help other kids deal with similar sadness. Her video, "A Hole in My Heart: A Child's Guide to Pet Loss" was produced in partnership with the Colorado State University Veterinary Teaching Hospital as a resource for its webpage (http://www.ChildPetLoss.com).

As Sachin reported on the importance of his ongoing project—it's now been more than 5 years in operation—it is clear that the benefits of such an endeavor are measurable in both tangible and intangible terms:

> I am so fortunate and proud to say that I was part of the 2008–2009 Young Scholar Ambassador Program. Through it, I not only learned the skills necessary to start and maintain my community service project, but also skills like leadership and planning that have helped me in every area of my life. The Ambassador Program has helped me learn and practice what community service means and enabled me to continue to learn and grow as a human being. (Schwinger & Delisle, 2012, p. 17)

Marcel Proust said that "we don't receive wisdom; we must discover it for ourselves after a journey that no one can take for us or spare us." With the YAP and the many other similar opportunities available for gifted children (and others) to share both their minds and their hearts, the journey beyond the classroom in service to the community is beneficial to both the givers and the receivers.

PINEAPPLES DON'T HAVE SLEEVES

Just when I got you all uplifted and enthusiastic about the possibilities that await gifted children as they explore their intellectual, emotional, and altruistic selves, I come along as the pin to burst your balloon. Yes, it's our nation's biggest educational albatross that is next discussed: the business (and it is BIG business!) of standardized testing and its negative effects on virtually everyone involved—kids, parents, and educators.

Let's begin with the cryptic title of this section: "Pineapples Don't Have Sleeves." In 2012, one of the questions in New York's eighth-grade English assessment involved a twist on the Aesop fable of the race between the tortoise and the hare. In this case, the hare was not racing a tortoise, but a talking pineapple. In the reading passage, the eighth graders learn that the other animals watching the race assumed that the pineapple had a trick up his sleeve that would enable him (who knew that pineapples were gender specific?) to outrun the hare. However, when the pineapple just stood there and did nothing, the animals ate him. The moral of the story? Pineapples don't have sleeves.

After reading this nonsensical passage that is presented as legitimate, students are asked to answer six multiple-choice questions, including which animal was wisest and why the animals ate the pineapple. Many eighth graders assumed the "wisest" question was a trick, as owls are touted as being wise and the owl is the animal who spouted out the tale's moral. As to why the pineapple got eaten, the two equally logical choices were because the animals were hungry or they were simply annoyed at the pineapple's behavior. As one gifted eighth grader responded when asked about this reading passage and questions, "I thought I was getting it wrong. I was second-guessing myself because it's so ridiculous."

This tale of pineapple woe was reported in *The New York Times* (Hartocollis, 2012) and, lo and behold, it was discovered that this same set of questions—or similar variations—also appeared on standardized tests in Delaware, Arkansas, Illinois, and Alabama. The test designer and distributor was not some fly-by-night operator, but the Pearson Corporation, one of the nation's largest producers of assessment instruments used worldwide. And even though the New York State Commissioner of Education later eliminated the pineapple passage from the students' tests scores, the damage had been done. As noted educator Deborah Meier stated in this same *New York Times* article, this pineapple fiasco is just "an outrageous example of what's true of most of the items on any test, it's just blown up larger" (Hartocollis, 2012, p. 2).

Perhaps more than any other philosophical, definitional, or organizational headwind confronting gifted learners, the strongest gust of all comes from the standardized testing movement that has taken over virtually every public school in America. Let's examine some of the reasons that the high-stakes testing movement (HST) has such negative impact on all students, including those who are gifted.

#1: THE COST

According to an analysis on the amount of money spent on K–12 assessments in America (Chingos, 2012) the total annual estimate is "upwards of roughly $1.7 billion" (p. 1). Although Chingos (2012) tried to mitigate this amount by stating that "this seemingly large number amounts to only one-quarter of one percent of annual K–12 education spending" (p. 1), there is no arguing that this is a ton of money that schools could use for other, more legitimate purposes—like teaching supplies or smaller class sizes. And because this is an *annual* cost that *doesn't even include* assessment costs that individual states or local school districts mandate (for example, ACT or SAT testing subsidies provided to students or state-endorsed proficiency tests), the cost to educational quality is exacerbated even more.

#2: TEST QUALITY . . . OR LACK THEREOF

The absurdity of the "pineapple passage" is just one of a countless number of examples of spurious ways that our children's intellectual capacity and achievement are being measured. And things are bound to get worse before they get better, as the adoption of the Common Core is going to require that *new* assessments be developed. The urge to get these tests into print *just as the Common Core standards are being introduced to teachers and students*, means that the cart will once again be placed in front of the horse: We'll be measuring student growth before we even have a chance to determine if the new Common Core curricula are worthwhile. So, until then, can't states just use the assessment instruments that many of them have been using all along? To cite Chingos (2012) on this point, "the quality of tests in many states is not high enough for high-stakes purposes such as teacher evaluation" (p. 2). So all of the billions of dollars that states spent on developing assessment tools years ago to meet the requirements of the now-dying NCLB legislation? I guess if the tests' quality isn't there now, it wasn't there then, either.

To the student assessment conundrum comes another wrinkle: Although 45 states and the District of Columbia had signed on initially to adopt the tests developed by one of two corsortia (Smarter Balanced and Partnership for Assessment of Readiness for College and Careers [PARCC]), that number had dwindled to 27 by 2014 (Gewertz & Ujifusa, 2014). For a variety of reasons—including cost, politics, and the required use of technology to administer the assessments—states have opted out and will, instead, use a smorgasbord of at least 19 different tests (Gewertz & Ujifusa, 2014). This collection of myriad new assessments caused James W. Pellegrino (who serves on the technical-advisory boards of the Smarter Balanced and PARCC) to conclude that this trend "moves us back closer to where we were under No Child Left Behind" (Gewertz & Ujifusa, 2014, p. 16). Pellegrino may be right—or not—but his observation is just one more indicator of the need to delay these Common Core assessments until they have had a chance to be implemented fully.

#3: LOSS OF INSTRUCTIONAL TIME

Diane Ravitch is no fan of gifted child education. However, when it comes to noting the loss of instructional time due to our addiction to testing, she is in the gifted kid's corner. She noted in 2012 that most schools begin the year with a week or so of testing to get a baseline on student achievement levels. Instead of then assessing at the end of the school year to see how well students have learned, we assess a few weeks later . . . and a few weeks after that, most often to discover those students whose learning is proceeding at a slower pace than desired. Those kids who aced the initial testing at the beginning of the school year? They still have to sit through tedious, repetitive assessments that tell us nothing new about these students' abilities or competencies that we didn't know already. Ravitch noted that the amount of time spent on assessment instead of instruction is *9 weeks*—that's one quarter of each school year. And because no instruction is going on while students are being assessed, gifted students continue to do what they are, sadly, very used to doing: sitting and waiting.

#4: TEACHING TO THE TEST

Ask any teacher if there is pressure to prepare students to do well on standardized tests and the answer will likely be "yes." As Lloyd Bond (2004) reported in a Carnegie Foundation article, "the temptation to tailor and restrict instruction to only that which will be tested is almost irresistible" (p. 1). That's not to say that teachers would choose to teach to the test—but in this era of accountable everything, learning often takes a back seat to test preparation. What gets lost in the process are several things: a comprehensive understanding of subject matter, a lack of opportunity to pursue creative or critical thinking, and the time to explore topics or subjects not covered on the tests—all of which are aspects of learning that attract the attention of gifted students. One can only hope that the new Common Core content standards will be broad enough that teaching to the test will be less of an issue in 5 years than it is today.

#5: CHEATING, AT THE TOP

In the Atlanta Public Schools, former Superintendent Beverly Hall and 35 other educators were indicted in 2013 for a cheating scandal that rippled across the national headlines. Facing fines of several million dollars and jail terms of up to 45 years, these educators are accused of changing student test scores to show how much their schools were improving from one year to the next. Not long before this scandal broke, Superintendent Hall had received a $500,000 bonus for shepherding this "success" and had been selected by the American

> Adults—educators, politicians, parents—need to begin engaging, rather than limiting, the academic potential of children. We, as a society, should value a student's ability to thrive in complex situations rather than his or her ability to answer a multiple-choice question. We should encourage students to scrutinize the world around them, to explore the landscape of the unimagined, and to bring the impossible to life. We must facilitate, rather than regulate, our students' pursuits to help them establish a better future. That is our duty.
>
> *Adam Hogue, 2013 graduate, Harvard University, Cambridge, MA*

Association of School Administrators as its "Superintendent of the Year." As reported in the *Washington Post*, "the refusal of Beverly Hall and her top administrators to accept anything other than satisfying targets created an environment where achieving the desired end result was more important than the students' education" (Strauss, 2013, p. 1).

And Atlanta is not alone, as Strauss also reported that, since 2009, cheating scandals have been confirmed in 37 states and the District of Columbia, affecting both large urban districts like New York City and Los Angeles and smaller communities, like Dougherty County (GA) Schools, where 49 educators (including 11 principals) were implicated in a widespread cheating scandal.

One could argue that gifted students are less victimized than lower performing students whose parents are being told great things about their children's success that are, in fact, lies. However, when a system of education is set up where those charged with preserving the sanctity of our kids' minds feel pressured to go to any lengths to show progress—in these cases, artificial progress—then every child loses out on a legitimate education.

A CHANGE IN THE AIR?

What was educationally significant and hard to measure has been replaced by what is educationally insignificant and easy to measure. So now we measure how well we taught what isn't worth learning.—Arthur Costa

In February 2013, a group of high school teachers in the Seattle Public Schools decided to boycott the administration of the Measures of Academic Progress (MAP) test to their classes. Given three times each year (in addition to two other state-mandated tests), the MAP was perceived by the protesting teachers to be a meaningless test that was not tied to the state curriculum. Teachers at two other Seattle high schools also decided to sit out the test. These teachers were told by school administrators that if they refused to administer the MAP they would each face a 10-day suspension. Still, the teachers held their ground. The end result? No protesting teacher was disciplined at all and, in fact, the school district decided to modify its testing structure, limiting the MAP to ninth graders who were below grade level in reading. Similar testing boycotts—these led by students—took place in Portland, OR, and in Providence, RI, where students went so far as to cover themselves in fake blood to protest being treated like zombies by being forced to take meaningless exams (Dornfield, 2013).

On a larger scale, a resolution calling for a reduction on high-stakes testing has been adopted by more than 86% of Texas school boards, affecting 91% of the K–12 students of the Lone Star State (Schaeffer, 2012). A version of this resolution has since been adapted by FairTest, a national organization promoting fair and open testing (http://www.fairtest.org) and cosponsored by such organizations as the Asian American Legal Defense and Education Fund, the National Education Association, and the United Church of Christ. Specifically, the FairTest (2012) resolution calls for these changes:

> RESOLVED that (your organization name) calls on the governor, state legislature and state education boards and administrators to reexamine public school accountability systems in this state, and to develop a system based on multiple forms of assessment which does not require extensive standardized testing, more accurately reflects the broad range of student learning, and is used to support students and improve schools; and
>
> RESOLVED, that (your organization name) calls on the U.S. Congress and Administration to overhaul the Elementary and Secondary Education Act (currently known as the "No Child Left Behind Act"), reduce the testing mandates, promote multiple forms of evidence of student learning and school quality in accountability, and not mandate any fixed

role for the use of student test scores in evaluating educators. (para. 11–12)

In 2013, Randi Weingarten, leader of the American Federation of Teachers, was another voice who sounded a clarion call to put a temporary stop on high-stakes testing. "We aren't saying teachers shouldn't be evaluated. We're not saying there shouldn't be standardized tests. We're talking about a moratorium on consequences in these transitional years" of implementing the Common Core State Standards (Bryant, 2013, p. 1). As an alternative, Weingarten called for a plan where frontline teachers would have time to field test the new assessments, gathering data on how well these assessments mesh with the new standards, without fear of reprisals from the high-stakes testing advocates who would moan about students' low test scores.

Weingarten's plan makes sense for both teachers and students, for how absurd is it to expect accurate assessments for curricula that have not yet been implemented fully? Apparently, she is not alone in her thinking, as shortly after her pronouncement, a group of organizations called the Learning First Alliance endorsed her testing moratorium. Including groups such as the American Association of School Administrators, the American School Counselor Association, Phi Delta Kappan International, and the National Parent Teacher Association, the Learning First Alliance represents more than 10 million parents, educators, and policy makers (Strauss, 2013b). Quite a powerful coalition of voices asking for the same thing: common sense thinking with regard to valid and reliable student assessments.

Sometimes, though, the most effective voice is a single one—in this case, a parent who also happens to be a school administrator.

Superintendent John Kuhn, from a small school district in Texas, testified in 2011 to the Public Education Committee of the Texas House of Representatives on behalf of a bill that would put a 2-year moratorium on standardized testing across the state, poignantly stating his rationale:

Testing has turned the adventure of education into something that feels more like an assembly line . . .

because student creativity is being sacrificed in favor of standardization, because scores are used to unfairly punish schools and teachers that embrace the neediest students.

So my dilemma is this: I would prefer that my son not participate in this test(ing) to avoid the weaponization of his data, and the perversion of his education. People say ending testing will water down education. I see test prep as watering down education. (Strauss, 2011, para. 5)

Indeed, these calls to action are already having a positive impact, as the vast majority of states have received waivers from the U.S. Department of Education from NCLB's onerous and unrealistic standards. Instead, other forms of documentation to show how well students are performing in school will be designed and used by individual states. It remains to be seen if these alternate assessments will be more sensible and usable or simply more of the same packaged a wee bit differently. Pessimist that I sometimes am when it comes to educational changes, I'm guessing the latter.

The cost we pay for investing so heavily on data instead of the dividends of student learning as measured by the joy of experiencing something new and exciting in the classroom is encapsulated well by Marc Prensky (2014), who reminds us that

we spend so much time and effort looking at test scores, averages, and other petty measurements of "learning" that we have little time or energy left to focus on who our students are (or are not) as individuals, what they love and hate, or what drives them. We shouldn't be surprised, then, if they become people we do not like or respect, or if we have concerns about their potential contributions to society. (p. 36)

Indeed, the stakes are that great. When we lose sight of the ultimate purpose of curriculum and instruction—to make our students more reflective and compassionate people—we lose the essence of what education can and should be: the primary vehicle for teaching our kids to make their generation better and more aware than our own. Am I discouraged by this absurd turn toward testing at all costs? Of course I am. But I do have hope, and it lies herein: I believe that the greatest change will come from this current generation of K–12 students who are bone-tired of the overreliance on standardized testing in today's schools. They have been the victims of this political barrage of purposeless tests and, I predict, will rise up when *their own* children enroll in schools and say, in effect, "not on my watch." As a result, the Pearson Corporation (and other test developers) may lose some business—and I'm fine with that. Because when you consider the alternative—that teachers will have several more weeks each year to teach and students to learn—the gains to be had will surely be great.

CHAPTER 8

THE BIG PICTURE

FITTING GIFTED CHILD EDUCATION INTO THE BROADER EDUCATIONAL LANDSCAPE

I don't think homeschoolers need to be brought back into the system. The fact that they are opting out will cause the public schools to make adjustments or lose students (and money). The reasons I opted out are that in school there is little room for creativity, original thinking, or independent learning. In high school (I spent a year there), I learned almost nothing but was forced to spend hours doing homework on the order of worksheets. I think there should be fewer worksheets and lectures taken directly out of the textbook and more discussion and independent reading, like is done in college. (Schultz & Delisle, 2012, p. 87)

The above quote, from a 16-year-old gifted girl, is a sad indictment of a 21st-century student being taught with 19th-century methods. She is not alone in her plight, as evidenced by the ever-increasing number of K–12 gifted students (and others) who are opting out of standard education and either being homeschooled, attending a virtual academy or charter school, or using vouchers to attend a private school. These options came into existence for one overwhelming reason: the day-to-day practices in the majority of America's schools are based more on the past than on the future. Students want out; they want something more than yesteryear's lessons and textbooks.

This final chapter will provide a blueprint that could serve to guide the education of gifted students into some new and important directions. There are many stakeholders in making the changes outlined here, both inside and outside of education, and unless and until there is a wholesale shift in both our attitudes and practices in support of gifted students, we shall continue to be "a nation deceived" into believing it is serving its most capable students well and wisely.

LET'S START AT THE STATE LEVEL

Although most educational decisions made in America are done at the school district level, those local practices are determined, to a considerable degree, by particular state laws and regulations that have been adopted by legislators and "fleshed out" by the policy wonks in charge of drawing up the rules and regulations for implementation. That being the case, it is most likely that gifted children's needs will be met if school districts and colleges of education are *told* what they must do, at a minimum, in response to the needs of gifted learners. These "to-do's" need not be long, but they must contain the elements described in the next sections.

TO-DO #1: TRAIN TEACHER CANDIDATES ABOUT GIFTED STUDENTS

States must require that every teacher candidate be made aware of the special needs of gifted students. Most gifted education specialists will have at least some college-level coursework regarding the characteristics and learning needs of gifted students. However, most gifted students spend the majority of their time in a regular classroom environment, and their teachers may know very little about who gifted kids are and what to do to challenge them; indeed, only six states require that every teacher candidate receive such information, and even that is likely to be minimal. By using the Knowledge and Skills Standards in Gifted and Talented Education for all teachers developed jointly by NAGC and CEC-TAG (2006), university-level course instructors will receive the guidance they need in presenting information to teacher candidates about who gifted kids are and how their needs can best be met.

The fate of our nation's brightest children rests with awareness—outside the field of gifted education. Instruction and strategies on which we have previously hung our hats for the gifted are now being implemented for all students. Up comes the floor; so, too, must the ceiling rise. We are a nation of rescue; our money and efforts are focused on success for the strugglers. While this is a worthy focus, it reduces effort and resources for our gifted students. Our nation's gifted children are desperate for an awareness that will create a visible critical need seen by all citizens.

Jan Fall, changing gifted lives across the country for more than 30 years

TO-DO #2: REQUIRE AND FUND IDENTIFICATION AND EDUCATION OF GIFTED STUDENTS

States must require and fund *the identification and legitimate education of gifted students in grades K–12.* As was stated earlier, only 29 states now require that gifted children be served in their school environment. And even when they *are* served, the amount and quality of instruction varies considerably from district to district. By adopting legislation requiring that gifted students be identified and served, states will be taking an important step in securing a legitimate education for gifted students. The two most important words in this recommendation are these: "and fund." For if states do not provide the financial wherewithal to educate gifted children and those who serve them, such an unfunded mandate is nothing more than window dressing—a superficial and meaningless presentation designed to create a favorable impression.

TO-DO #3: LET STUDENTS
GRADE THE TEACHERS

Include student assessments of their teachers' effectiveness as a part of the teacher evaluation process. A decade ago, Harvard University economist Ronald Ferguson wondered what would happen if the people most aware of a teacher's in-classroom behavior—the students— were asked to evaluate their teachers' effectiveness. His findings were incredibly consistent among the 250,000 students surveyed, even among kindergarten students. As reported by Ripley (2012) "if you asked kids the right questions, they could identify, with uncanny accuracy, their most—and least—effective teachers" (p. 90). Students were able to determine in which classrooms they worked hard, paid attention, and corrected their mistakes; classrooms they enjoyed being in and where they believed the teacher cared about them. They could also identify the classrooms in which *none* of these positive aspects of learning were found. The school superintendent in one district surveyed commented: "we knew the relationships that teachers build with students were important . . . but seeing proof of it in the survey results made a big difference. We found the results to be extremely helpful" (Ripley, 2012, p. 91). In 2011, the Memphis school system became the first in the nation to tie student survey results to their annual reviews, accounting for 5% of a teacher's evaluation—a proportion that will go up in future years. And in Chicago, beginning in 2013, student survey results will count for 10% of a teacher's evaluation.

Gifted students are uncannily shrewd when it comes to determining which teachers are worth listening to, and which are not. But by actually using their precise impressions to determine, to some degree, a teacher's effectiveness, we are providing them a valid voice in evaluating their educations' worth. As one surveyed student at Washington, DC's McKinley High School, a STEM-focused magnet school, said, "they should've done this since I was in 8th grade" (Ripley, 2012, p. 90).

TO-DO #4: NO MORE TESTS . . . FOR 3 YEARS

Institute a 3-year moratorium on statewide standardized testing. In the previous chapter, several prominent educators presented their rationale for adopting a testing moratorium. In their stead, students would be evaluated by end-of-course tests designed by their teachers, as well as several other options that more directly link student assessment with the curriculum they are taught. Therefore, instead of arguing a valid point once again, let me simply present some facts, figures, and commentary that bolster the case for a testing moratorium. In doing so, I'll return to Texas.

The supposed "Texas Miracle" that George W. Bush proclaimed when the state he governed first imposed standardized testing in the late 1990s became more like a "Texas Debacle," as the supposed gains in test scores by minority children and kids from poverty did not hold up over time—and may never have been real at all. Still, he used these errant data as his platform to launch NCLB when he became President of the United States. In Texas, back in 2009, the state decided to design another set of standardized tests to replace earlier ones that had been widely criticized. The result: harder tests with fewer students passing them. So, in response, Texas entered into a $500 million contract with Pearson to develop new tests, a figure that is projected to balloon to $1.1 billion by 2015 (Rapaport, 2013). As Pearson was getting rich beyond belief, Governor Rick Perry slashed the state's education budget by $5.4 billion, and is looking for even more cuts in the future. The response: Even the Perry-appointed state education commissioner stated that testing had become a "perversion of the original intent" and needed to be scaled back (he has since resigned his post).

This former commissioner found some unlikely allies: Dozens of Republican legislators from across the state, as evidenced by resolutions from more than 800 school boards calling to place a statewide moratorium on testing. Why do I call these allies "unlikely"? Because an end to rampant testing is often seen as a liberal, leftwing view. Now, it makes enough fiscal sense that even in the reddest-of-red states, the idea is gaining traction. As Rapaport concluded, "(Texas) did more than any other state to bring the country into an era of Number 2 pencils and filling in bubbles. It might also be the state that leads us out" (2013, p. 1).

Now *that* would be a genuine "Texas Miracle!"

LOCAL LEVEL SOLUTIONS

Let's return to the idea of "exam schools," the 165 public high schools that Chester Finn and Jessica Hockett (2012) highlighted as being exemplars of the best in education. California has nine exam schools, the city of Chicago alone has eight, the state of Maine has one, . . . and 19 states have none at all. Ranging in size from 68 students (University Preparatory High School in Visalia, CA) to 4,947 (Brooklyn Technical High School in New York), these exemplary schools educate less than 1% of all secondary school students in America, a figure that Finn and Hockett found appallingly low. Calling students who attend these schools "the seedlings of tomorrow's intellectual crops" (p. 200), the authors contended that tens of thousands of other students are in dire need of such high-powered academic options. To wit, "[Exam schools] aren't the only way to incentivize or educate high-ability youngsters in the K–12 world, but they're a valuable part of a comprehensive strategy that the United States neglects at its peril" (p. 201).

"Comprehensive strategy" is little more than a pipedream in most school districts across America when it comes to educating its gifted youth. So even if dozens of new exam schools are unlikely to open without a groundswell of commitment and financial support from government, businesses, and philanthropic agencies (more on this later), the idea of whole-school excellence for gifted students is within our grasp; those seedlings of tomorrow's intellectual crops can, indeed, be nurtured. In Chapter 7, I explained several ways to define, identify, and serve gifted children's educational needs. They are outlined in the following section in a more condensed form.

SOLUTION #1: CREATE A PHILOSOPHY FOR THE GIFTED PROGRAM

Before a gifted program is ever begun, develop a philosophy statement that is consistent with the school district's mission. Most school districts' mission statements will offer some grandiose words about how "every student will be allowed to achieve to his or her personal potential." Fine and dandy. Now, put your money where your mouth is and include gifted students' needs in the equation. The place to do this is in a gifted program philosophy statement, examples of which can be found in Delisle and Lewis (2003).

SOLUTION #2: ESTABLISH A TOTAL-CHILD DEFINITION OF GIFTEDNESS

Establish a definition of giftedness that encompasses the totality of a child's existence. The newest NAGC definition of giftedness focuses so strongly on "talent development" that the essence of the gifted child as something other than an academic specimen is lost. An "IQ-alone" definition is as limiting as would be any definition that does not have some "wiggle room" for giftedness that is expressed in various ways. And a definition that focuses only on the emotional parts of being gifted runs the risk of being so amorphous that identification is left more to opinion than analysis. Examine the many definitions that exist and determine which one best fits your community. This is one area where uniformity will never be achieved, so locate a definition you are most comfortable with and plan your identification and school programs from there. My suggestion for a cohesive definition of giftedness appeared in Chapter 7.

SOLUTION #3: CAST A WIDE NET FOR IDENTIFYING GIFTED LEARNERS

Design an identification system that is cognizant of both typical and atypical gifted learners. As mentioned earlier, the muckiest part of gifted program is the identification process, so a wide net must be cast to discover talent even when it is latent. Students from poverty, students of color, twice-exceptional kids, and those whom teachers call "smart, but lazy" are prime candidates to be overlooked when the gifted screening process begins. *Don't let this happen.* Too, there are many gifted students whose parents don't "know the ropes" when it comes to the identification process, so make sure the timelines and procedures are readily available to them. Unless a gifted program's identification process is broad-based and flexible, cries of "elitism" might, in fact, be accurate.

SOLUTION #4: PROVIDE LOTS OF EDUCATIONAL OPTIONS

Develop a menu of educational options that is as diverse as a smorgasbord. Of the 87,000 seventh and eighth graders annually who take the SAT for "practice" (or entrance into a gifted summer program), 22,000 of them score at the level of college-bound high school seniors (Thornburg, 2004). Do you think that a one-day-per-week gifted program will meet their academic needs sufficiently? Doubtful, at best. These "varsity" level gifted students will need access to acceleration in many of its forms, while a "junior varsity" gifted student who is operating 1 or 2 years above grade level may be intellectually satisfied with content enrichment and some independent study projects. One size doesn't fit all, in blue jeans or education, so be certain to make your gifted program offerings as diverse as the students themselves.

SOLUTION #5: DON'T FORGET ABOUT PRIMARY AND SECONDARY STUDENTS

Plan for a gifted student's entire K–12 career, not just those grade levels where an extant gifted program is in place. In districts that offer a weekly pull-out program in grades 3–6, it is easy to forget that these same gifted students exist in first and eighth grades, too. A comprehensive gifted program plan that acknowledges the presence of students' giftedness across all grade levels will help ensure that the gaps in learning are few. VanTassel-Baska (2012) recommended that it is critical to define what differentiation will look like across the grade levels and subject areas, and stated that

> a good strategy to begin the task is to design down from Advanced Placement options and/or the International Baccalaureate program. This will solidify an emphasis on higher-level thinking in each domain as well as align well to the highest level of curriculum available to gifted learners in most school districts. (p. 223)

Leaving this articulation of curriculum to chance is like starting a 2,000 mile trip without a map: You'll end up somewhere, but not likely where or how you intended to proceed.

SOLUTION #6: GIVE GIFTED STUDENTS TEACHERS WHO UNDERSTAND THEM

Assign gifted students to teachers who get them and like them. Perhaps the most important consideration of all, this element of understanding and acceptance of giftedness by a teacher is essential to a positive student outcome. Sadly, too often principals assign gifted students to teachers based on a "fairness" doctrine—everyone gets a few gifted kids—or on seniority, where the veteran teachers get the gifted kids because they are "easier to teach." My advice? Assign gifted students only to teachers who have taken the time to learn who they are and how to teach them by taking coursework or professional development opportunities on giftedness and differentiation. To do otherwise invites all manner of mistreatment, such as this, as reported by a gifted teacher recalling her high school years:

> There may be rules about serving gifted children, but there is no enforcement. All of this creates an environment in which gifted students feel as though they are not valued or challenged. My history teacher would often read my essays as examples. Not only was I embarrassed, but I did not receive any instruction.

The teacher didn't care whether I was growing as a learner. (Hargrove, 2013, p. 79)

Such educational malpractice should never be tolerated yet, in the case of gifted students who are assigned to teachers who neither know nor care about their special learning needs, it happens far too often.

SOLUTION #7: THINK BIG

Think big . . . VERY big. Stephen Schroeder-Davis, whose work I referenced in Chapter 3, has worked with gifted students for 40 years or so, giving him more than ample time to reflect on what we do well, and what we can do better, in educating gifted students. Of particular importance, yet often neglected, is a focus on intellectualism in deference to a data-driven educational structure that focuses on the lowest common denominators of learning: passing standardized tests. Schroeder-Davis (2013) asked if, instead, we can devote our time to inculcating the following qualities in gifted students:

- ◇ *intellectual humility*: being conscious of the limits of one's knowledge, sensitivity to bias, and prejudice
- ◇ *intellectual courage*: resisting the urge to uncritically accept what we have "learned" and having the courage to be true to our thoughts, even when nonconformity is punished
- ◇ *intellectual empathy*: the ability to reconstruct accurately the viewpoints and reasoning of others and the willingness to recall past occasions when we were wrong—especially when we were convinced we were right
- ◇ *intellectual integrity*: holding one's self to the same rigorous standards of evidence and proof to which one holds one's antagonists
- ◇ *intellectual perseverance*: being conscious of the need to use intellectual insights and truths in spite of difficulties, obstacles, and frustrations
- ◇ *faith in reason*: confidence that, in the long run, one's own higher interests, and those of humankind at large, will be best served by reason. (p. 8)

These elements of learning and living are gleaned from the Foundation for Critical Thinking (2011) and could serve as the guiding principles that underlie the curricular efforts we practice with gifted youth. In doing so, both cognitive and affective muscles are stretched and students, along with their teachers at home and in school, become both more capable and caring. What could be better?

Ann Isaacs (1971), founder of the National Association for Gifted Children, noted that "Only a community that cares about its gifted children deserves to have them; only one that fosters their development can expect to see its fruition" (p. iv). More than a generation after those words were written, America is still educationally short-sheeting its gifted students. The need for them to grow and stretch is as unfulfilled today as it was when Ann Isaacs founded NAGC in 1954.

Everyone has creative potential! Yes, we are all born with the capacity for creative activity. Just think of young children. They explore, question, wonder, experiment, express, decorate, elaborate, renovate, remodel, and renew . . . every day. For creatively gifted children, these activities are as essential as eating and breathing. They bring life and nourishment to the creative child's soul. Yet research shows that by fourth grade, this creative outlook begins to dwindle, likely due to an emphasis on standardized testing and one-right-answer responses. We must change this trend by purposely integrating and celebrating creativity—and multiple possible responses—within our schools.

Susan Daniels, Associate Professor,
California State University, San Bernadino, CA

SO WHAT?

After all that we do to try to meet the needs of gifted learners, the most essential question of all remains this simple one: "So what?" Did our efforts matter? (How do we know?) Did the various gifted program elements pan out the way we hoped they would? (What evidence do you have that says so?) Are our gifted children continuing to grow and learn? (Who determines this . . . and how?) These are not easy questions to answer—no bubble sheet/test exists that can measure intellectual honesty or personal determination to learn—yet they are the most fundamental questions of all. You will find answers to these questions only through observations and interviews, self-reflection based on self-reporting, and a willingness to change direction when the partners in learning—students, educators, parents—agree that a course correction is needed.

If a gifted program evaluation focuses on whether students already at the top academically have grown even further, we have missed a major opportunity to see education from a larger perspective—a more important and personal perspective. Gather numeric data if you must until the bean counters are satisfied, but then return to an evaluation that assesses something more vital: gifted children's continued willingness to learn thanks to the efforts that others have taken on their behalf.

BUSINESS AND PHILANTHROPY: PARTNERS IN WAITING

John Gowan, an early researcher in the counseling of gifted children, once said that the idea of educating gifted children in America is a "passionless issue in a society geared to emergencies." For all the reasons elaborated upon in *Dumbing Down America*—the generally held belief that gifted kids will make it on their own or that they all come from families capable of supporting them financially and otherwise—the needs of gifted children have been virtually ignored by major corporations and philanthropic institutions. The irony of this is that critics of the public education system in America bemoan our low standing in academics compared to other nations, yet the very kids who could be the true academic high-flyers with just a little bit more corporate attention—gifted kids—are largely bypassed when the checks are being written.

There are some notable exceptions, of course. As highlighted earlier, the Davidson Institute for Talent Development and the Jack Kent Cooke Foundation have missions that focus specifically on gifted children. Also, the Templeton Foundation (http://www.templeton. org) underwrote the costs of the important report on acceleration, *A Nation Deceived*, and provided $2.5 million to Johns Hopkins and other universities to develop Cogito.org, an online community that connects young thinkers around the world in the areas of math and science. In addition, there are other, smaller scale not-for-profits like the already mentioned Institute for Educational Advancement (http://www.educationaladvancement.org), which supports student scholarships and offers summer programs for gifted students, as well as the Gifted Education Foundation (http://www.iamgifted.org) that offers scholarships and mentorships to low-income gifted students who would be first-generation college graduates.

Yet these organizations, as important as they are for the students who benefit from their services, are limited in their scope. They are certainly no match for the Ford Foundation, one of the nation's largest, which distributed $413 million in grants in 2011. Considering that the Ford Foundation's goal is to "look for fresh thinking and innovative people and organizations" (see the grants page on its website, http://www.fordfoundation.org/Grants, for more), you'd think that gifted education would fit this bill perfectly. However (and disturbingly), a search of their database using the term "gifted children" yields this reply: "Sorry, no grants match the search criteria." And the world's largest private foundation, the Gates Foundation, with an endowment of $36 billion, has been largely absent when it comes to supporting gifted children. Although two of their targeted areas are "college-ready education" and "postsecondary success," a search of their website for grants aimed at gifted children yields but two results: funding the development of a university in Bangladesh for gifted women and establishing a scholarship program at Cambridge University in England.

Corporate America, too, is mostly absent when it comes to funding programs specifically in support of gifted children. In 2012, *Forbes* magazine listed the five largest corporations in America as these:

1. ExxonMobil
2. WalMart
3. Chevron

4.   Conoco-Phillips

5.   General Motors

Each of these corporations has a philanthropic adjunct that distributes, collectively, billions of dollars in grants annually, with ExxonMobil, Conoco-Phillips, and General Motors focusing more on education than do WalMart or Chevron. However, as generous as these corporations are, a look into the types of projects they fund yields the typical recipients: math and science education, vocational education, early childhood assistance to at-risk young learners, and small-scale teacher grants to buy basic school supplies. Gifted children? Nowhere to be found specifically as a priority population.

Here's what needs to happen: The major associations that advocate for gifted children, spearheaded by NAGC, have to get their houses in order and invest in a collective effort to convince corporate America that gifted kids are worth saving. Whether foundations fund gifted education options out of self-interest, genuine belief in the cause, or a combination of the two, money is money. This focus on raising both awareness and dollars has been too limited in past years, as the national gifted associations have generally asked for donations from the associations' membership rolls. We need more. We need bigger. And the best organizations that can do this are those whose commitment to gifted children goes back decades—such as those discussed in Chapter 6. Specifically, a collective of gifted education organizations needs to hire a director of development whose salary will be paid, proportionately, by each member of this network. By approaching possible donors with a strong, common message who represent gifted children, families, and educators nationwide, the chances of funding success are greater than if each association acted alone—or, as is common now, not at all. Who knows? Maybe some corporations or philanthropies will work hand-in-hand with states and districts that wish to increase the number of exam schools in our nation. Or since university professors have "endowed chairs" occupied by the most effective and respected of their faculty, why not endow a gifted teacher at a local elementary or high school? The "ExxonMobil Gifted Educator of Hoboken High School"—it has a good ring to it, don't you think?

It's time to put the typical rivalry among organizations with a similar mission aside and act as a united voice for gifted children. To continue along the same old-same old path we have trod for decades will yield only more of what we already have: small change in a bountiful harvest of funding dollars.

ENTER THE FEDS . . . AGAIN?

An ongoing national effort to identify and serve gifted and creative students has actually been underway since 1999. Initially funded with government and private sources to the tune of $76 million, this program gets additional yearly funding of $3.8 million, with the goal of locating and serving 14,000 more gifted students annually. With several multiyear strategic plans established with the help of an international team of educators and consultants, the latest plan has this as its goal by the year 2022: "To be a creative society with a critical mass of gifted and talented young leaders who are innovative, highly-educated and well-trained to support the sustained growth and prosperity of the Kingdom" (Dracup, 2011, para. 59).

Oh yeah . . . the Kingdom. This is not America's national plan for gifted children, it is Saudi Arabia's. The custodian of the two holy mosques, King Abdullah bin Abdulaziz served as the primary funder and first President of this endeavor, named "Mawhiba," the Arabic word for "gift or talent." Mawhiba (http://www.mawhiba.org) provides an array of services for both gifted boys and gifted girls, including scholarships to distinct schools; direct instruction in summer programs; competitions and awards for entrepreneurial endeavors; internships; an online support center that can be accessed by gifted students, their parents, and teachers; face-to-face counseling; and a customer service center that helps coordinate Mawhiba's many and varied activities. A school partnership initiative has also been established to help schools design and implement special programs for gifted students. Mawhiba has been called "the most comprehensive educational approach to nurturing high performance and creativity in the world" (Eyre, 2011,

p. 48) and its end goal is that the students who benefit from Mawhiba's services will become part of a knowledge-based society capable of producing, using, and disseminating knowledge. Mawhiba's students are already being very successful in their efforts, as evidenced by the stunning array of awards in plant sciences, biochemistry, molecular biology, medicine and health services, bioengineering, social/behavioral sciences, and more that they have garnered at the INTEL International Science and Engineering Fair between 2007–2014.

Meanwhile, back in the United States, not much is happening to support gifted kids at the national level. When the U.S. Congress eliminated funding for the Jacob K. Javits Gifted Education Act in 2010, it erased the only federally funded program aimed specifically at gifted children. But, to be honest, this was no great loss, for although the program did benefit some gifted students directly, it did more to fill the coffers of universities that collected millions of dollars, year after year, grant after grant, to fund projects that were seldom maintained once the funding stopped. Let's hope the new 2014 Javits funding doesn't make the same mistakes with its funding priorities. The Javits program was extremely limited in scope, especially in contrast with Mawhiba. Besides, the most money Javits ever received was $11.5 million in the year of its onset (2002), which is a mere pittance compared to what Mawhiba provides, and is even more miniscule when compared to the outlay of 11.5 *billion* federal dollars spent annually in America on children with disabilities.

In 2011, an NAGC-sponsored bill, the TALENT Act, was introduced in Congress but ended up garnering little support, with only six legislators signing on as cosponsors. Reintroduced in 2013 (and its fate still pending), the TALENT Act, in my humble opinion, is a weak "feel good" bill that would not create any new programs in support of gifted children nor would it be a separate authorization compelling school districts to do much of anything different for gifted students. Instead, it would tack on some minor adjustments to the Elementary and Secondary Education Act (also pending legislative approval), such as these:

⬦ permitting gifted education to be an "allowable" topic under the Rural Education Achievement Program,

Gifted children require programs constructed similarly to the most awesome amusement park roller coaster. Their ride through gifted programs should include opportunities to climb aboard with others or brave the action solo, options to ride beside adults or sit beside peers. Learning experiences must be packed with sudden turns, soaring heights, death-defying drops, and the occasional loop-de-loop. Program success should be measured by children's frequent chances to lean into learning, grip knowledge, and gain momentum toward personal development. When the program concludes, before running at full speed to the next attraction, the expressions on their faces must shout, "What a ride!"

Christine Dietz, Little Rock School District, Little Rock, AR

◇ directing the U.S. Secretary of Education to report to Congress and the public how states and districts are taking steps to close the achievement gap, and

◇ disseminating evidence-based best practices to improve the identification and instruction of gifted students.

In fact, the only requirements, should the TALENT Act pass, would be to ensure that *some* school staff had *some* training to identify and serve gifted students, and that schools receiving Title I funds would need to describe how they identify and serve gifted students. These are hardly robust requirements and would likely do little to enhance the education of gifted students in any noticeable ways.

We need to think bigger if we are going to be truly supportive of our nation's most capable youth—as big, in fact, as a nuclear attack submarine.

James Gallagher, one of our field's most recognized and accomplished scholars, proposed just such a plan. In an article titled "Educational Disarmament, and How to Stop It," Gallagher (2013) put forth a multipart proposal that would cost around $400 million over a 5-year period. Given that one nuclear submarine costs $8.2 billion to build, and that the U.S. Navy wishes to add 12 new ones to its already-impressive arsenal, could we not get by with 11 of these war machines and use one sixteenth of the money saved by not buying that 12th submarine for Gallagher's proposed program?

If so, here are what Gallagher's ideas would buy:

⬦ Research that would include new efforts in preschool programming, as well as initiatives in determining successful transitions from school to work. Further, a number of longitudinal studies could inform us as to what types of educational programs are most effective in serving gifted children.

⬦ A technology focus that would include ways to most effectively apply existing and emerging technologies in educational settings, with long-term trials assessing the effects of new technologies on learning. Several national centers on technical innovation would be established to study the interplay between technology and educational practices.

⬦ A curriculum development focus that funds teams of curricula specialists as well as establishing "centers and institutes where they work to design, test, and evaluate new content and procedures that will excite and motivate students with special gifts or talents" (p. 200).

⬦ Technical assistance to states that are having troubles with gifted dropouts, gifted kids with behavior problems, curriculum implementation, and other issues that require judicious tenacity to be resolved. Five technical centers to address these issues would be established. Commenting on the need for such centers, Gallagher asked, "What happens if a teacher or supervisor in distress calls an educational 911 for help—Does anyone answer?" (p. 201).

⬦ Demonstration centers that reward schools throughout the country that are successfully implementing problem-based learning, curriculum differentiation, STEM initiatives, International Baccalaureate programs, and other programs of high quality. Funds would be given to allow visitors to view the schools in operation and to provide short-term instruction on transferring this excellence to other educational settings.

⬦ Leadership training, including underwriting graduate programs needed to prepare gifted specialists who will administer these new initiatives. As Gallagher wrote, "advanced graduate students who take on these tasks should not be expected to pay for their total education any more than advanced medical students would be expected to pay for theirs" (p. 200).

As Gallagher observed, and rightly so: "If it is true that education represents the world's battleground of the 21st century, then the United States, with its budget cutbacks and recent criticism of educators, has been committing unilateral educational disarmament compared to other nations" (p. 197). His proposal, modest in comparison to the cost of one nuclear submarine, has the potential to do much greater good for our nation's gifted children, and for our nation as a whole, than any single piece of military equipment ever could.

THAT'S ALL, FOLKS!

It's been quite a journey, hasn't it? Approximately 60,000 words fill this book and most of them are dedicated to a single cause: improving the lives of gifted children through understanding, acceptance, and education. Throughout our history, we have had a love/hate relationship with the idea of giftedness. Thus, although we love the fruits of a gifted child's labors—a new theory unearthed, a memorable song written, a more complete understanding of the human psyche—our egalitarian-minded selves hate the thought of identifying some children as gifted and others as . . . well, not gifted. And even though we understand, in theory, the importance of providing gifted children with an excellent education, in practice we operate as if this will happen on its own, with little direct intervention that is regarded as essential, not peripheral, to their complete development.

This issue is well exemplified in the problems we face with respect to gifted children today. We are now going through a period of considerable interest in the able youngster. We went through a similar period in the 1920s. That earlier period was succeeded by an almost savage rejection of any measures designed for the gifted youngster and insistence on precisely the same treatment for all students.

Actually, the above paragraph should be written with quotation marks, as almost those exact words were written by John Gardner, in 1961, in his classic book *Excellence* (p. 115) which was referenced earlier and serves as the underlying foundation for this book's message. Indeed, Shakespeare was right: "What's past is prologue."

So keeping Gardner's message in mind, I have to wonder if 50 years from now, when my time on Earth will long have passed, someone will pick up a faded, dog-eared copy of this book as they prepare to write another book on the issue of gifted children in America. If that happens, I hope that that faraway author can use *Dumbing Down America* to reflect on how far we've come, instead of how far we yet have to go; that my book's contents will serve as nothing more than a relic filled with ancient references, each one more irrelevant than the next due to the progress we have made in understanding the importance of giving gifted children the attention they deserve; that the author writing in the year 2164 will read the following quote from a 14-year-old gifted child and find it to be a sad statement about a bygone era when gifted children were regarded with callous indifference:

> One of (my) biggest challenges is that programs and services for gifted kids are being eliminated. In my district, the fourth- and fifth-grade program was cut this year due to money issues—the teacher was laid off. Are they going to send the kids somewhere else? Or are we just going to get nothing? (Schultz & Delisle, 2012, p. 85)

Jeff, Morgan, and Justin, the three students whose personal stories opened this book, deserve more than . . . nothing. So does every gifted boy or girl you know who brought you to read this book in the first place.

For too long, genius *has* been denied and our nation *has* been deceived. With knowledge, tenacity, a strong collective voice, and a gifted child's needs at the forefront of your efforts, we *can* do better. Saving smart kids isn't a choice; it's an obligation.

REFERENCES

Aesopian. (2012). *Book review:* The Talent Code *by Daniel Coyle.* Retrieved from http://aesopian.com/1697/book-review-the-talent-code-by-daniel-coyle

Armstrong, T. (2009). *Multiple intelligences in the classroom.* Alexandria, VA: Association for Supervision and Curriculum Development.

Assouline, S., Colangelo, N., Lupowski-Shoplik, A., Lipscomb, J., & Forstadt, L. (2009). *The Iowa Acceleration Scale: A guide for whole-grade acceleration K–8.* Scottsdale, AZ: Great Potential Press

Berliner, D. C., & Biddle, B. J. (1995). *The manufactured crisis: Myths, fraud and the attack on America's public schools.* Reading, MA: Addison-Wesley.

Birch, B. A. (2012). *SC Gov Nikki Haley backs bill to block Common Core Standards.* Retrieved from http://www.educationnews.org/education-policy-and-politics/sc-gov-nikki-haley-backs-bill-to-block-common-core-standards

Bond, L. (2004). *Teaching to the test.* Retrieved from http://www.carnegiefoundation.org/perspectives/teaching-test

Bradley, D. (2012). Why Gladwell's 10,000-hour rule is wrong. *BBC Future.* Retrieved from http://bbc.com/future/story/ 2012/11/4

Branch, B. (2012, Summer). Khan Academy. *Gifted Education Communicator,* 38–40.

Branch, J. (2011). 5 teens who are helping others. *Family Circle.* Retrieved from http://www.familycircle.com/family-fun/vol unteering/5-teens-helping-others-online/?page=3

Brewer, D., Rees, D., & Argys, L. (1995). Detracking America's schools. *Phi Delta Kappan, 77,* 210–214.

Bromberg, M., & Theokas, C. (2014). *Falling out of the lead: Following high achievers through high school and beyond.* Washington, DC: The Education Trust.

Bryant, J. (2013). *Why we need a moratorium on the high stakes of Common Core testing.* Retrieved from http://nepc.colorado.edu/blog/why-we-need-moratorium-high-stakes-common-core-testing

Bui, S. A., Craig, S. G., & Imberman, S. A. (in press). Is gifted education a bright idea? Assessing the impact of gifted and talented programs on students. *American Economic Policy Journal.*

Case, S. (2012). Congress should pass the Start Up Act 2.0. *TechCrunch.* Retrieved from http://www.techcrunch.com/ 2012/06/15

Cavanaugh, S. (2004). Reagan's legacy: A Nation at Risk, boost for choice. *Education Week.* Retrieved from http://www.edweek.org/ew/articles/2004/16/40reagan.h23.html?qs=a_ nation_at_risk

Chen, M. (2010). *Education nation: Six leading edges of innovation.* San Francisco, CA: Jossey-Bass.

Chingos, M. M. (2012). *Strength in numbers: State spending on K–12 assessment systems.* Washington, DC: Brookings Institute.

Clark, B. (1997). *Growing up gifted.* Upper Saddle River, NJ: Prentice-Hall.

Colangelo, N., Assouline, S. G., & Gross, M. U. M. (2004). *A nation deceived: How schools hold back America's brightest students* (Vol. 1). Iowa City: The University of Iowa, The Connie Belin & Jacqueline N. Blank International Center for Gifted Education and Talent Development.

Collins, C. A., & Gan, L. (2013). *Does sorting students improve scores? An analysis of class composition* (National Bureau of Economic Research, Working Paper #18848). Retrieved from http://www.nber.org/papers/w18848

Council for Exceptional Children. (2007). *CEC's position on Response to Intervention: The unique role of special education and special educators.* Arlington, VA: Author.

Council for Exceptional Children, The Association for the Gifted. (2009). *Response to Intervention for gifted children.* Arlington, VA: Author.

Coyle, D. (2009). *The talent code: Greatness isn't born. It's grown. Here's how.* New York, NY: Bantam.

Dakos, K. (1995). *If you're not here, please raise your hand.* New York, NY: Aladdin Paperbacks.

Darling-Hammond, L. (2010). What we can learn from Finland's successful school reform. *NEA Today Online.* Retrieved from http://www.nea.org/home/40991.htm

Davidson Institute for Talent Development. (2006). *Does NCLB require that no child can get ahead?* Retrieved from http://www.davidsongifted.org/db/Articles_id_10361.aspx

Dayton, M. (2008). *The Senate site: Concern with the IB-Part II.* Retrieved from http://senatesite.com/blog/2008/05/concern-with-ib-part-ii.html

Delisle, D., & Delisle, J. (2011). *Building strong writers in middle school: Classroom-ready activities that inspire creativity and support state standards.* Minneapolis, MN: Free Spirit.

Delisle, J. (1996). Multiple intelligences: Convenient, simple, wrong. *Gifted Child Today, 19*(4), 20–21.

Delisle, J. (2003). *Do you know if gifted children are being served appropriately?* Retrieved from http://www.sengifted.org/archives/articles/do-we-know-if-gifted-children-are-being-served-appropriately

Delisle, J. (2012). *A defining moment.* Retrieved from http://www.hoagiesgifted.org/defining_moment.html

Delisle, J., & Lewis, B. A. (2003). *The survival guide for teachers of gifted kids.* Minneapolis, MN: Free Spirit.

Delisle, J. R. (1992). *Guiding the social and emotional development of gifted youth.* White Plains, NY: Longman.

Dornfield, A. (2013). *Seattle high school's teachers toss district test.* Retrieved from http://www.npr.org/2013/01/17/169620124/seattle-high-schools-teachers-toss-districts-test

Dracup, T. (2011). *Mawhiba: Gifted education in Saudi Arabia (Part one).* Retrieved from http://giftedphoenix.wordpress.com/2011/05/24/mawhiba-gifted-education-in-saudi-arabia-part-one

Dvorak, T. (2013). *Grant helps Idaho schools plug into online classes.* Retrieved from http://www.kboi2.com/news/local/grant-helps-Idaho-schools-plug-into-online-classes-194088691.html

Ericsson, K. A., Krampe, R. T., & Tesch-Romer, C. (1993). The role of deliberative practice in the acquisition of expert performance. *Psychological Review, 100,* 363–406.

Eyre, D. (2011). *Room at the top: Inclusive education for high performance.* London, England: Policy Exchange.

FairTest. (2012). *National resolution on high-stakes testing.* Retrieved from http://fairtest.org/national-resolution-high stakes-testing

Farkas, S., & Duffett, A. (2008). *High-achieving students in the era of NCLB: Results from a national teacher survey.* Washington, DC: Thomas B. Fordham Institute.

Federal Inventory of STEM Education Fast-Track Action Committee. (2011). *The federal science, technology, engineering, and mathematics (STEM) education portfolio.* Washington, DC: Office of the President of the United States.

Ferenstein, G. (2012). Why it's never mattered that America's schools 'lag' behind other countries. *TechCrunch.* Retrieved from http://techcrunch.com/2012/09/16/why-its-never-mattered-that-americas-schools-lag-behind-other-countries

Ferguson, C. (2009). Not every child is secretly a genius. *The Chronicle of Higher Education.* Retrieved from http://chronicle.com/article/Not-Every-Child-Is-Secretly-a/48001/

Ferguson, R. (2010). *Student perceptions of teaching effectiveness: Discussion brief.* Cambridge, MA: Harvard University, National Center for Teacher Effectiveness and the Achievement Gap Initiative.

Finn, C. (2012, Sept. 19). Young, gifted and neglected. *The New York Times,* A-29.

Finn, C. E., & Hockett, J. A. (2012). *Exam schools: Inside America's most selective public high schools.* Princeton, NJ: Princeton University Press.

Finn, K. (2007). Homeschooling with profoundly gifted kids. In K. Kay, D. Robson, & J. Fort (Eds.), *High IQ kids: Collected insights, information and personal stories from the experts* (pp. 179–185). Minneapolis, MN: Free Spirit.

Foundation for Critical Thinking. (2011). *Valuable intellectual traits*. Retrieved from http://www.criticalthinking.org/pages/valuable-intellectual-traits/528

Gagné, F. (1994). Are teachers really poor talent detectors?: Comments on Pegnato and Birch's (1959) study on the effectiveness and efficiency of various identification techniques. *Gifted Child Quarterly, 38,* 124–126.

Gagné, F. (2003). Transforming gifts into talents: The DMGT as a developmental theory. In N. Colangelo & G. A. Davis (Eds.), *Handbook of gifted education* (3rd ed., pp. 60–74). Boston, MA: Allyn & Bacon.

Gagné, F. (2004). A differentiated model of giftedness and talent (DMGT): Year 2000 update. *High Ability Studies, 15,* 119–147.

Galbraith, J., & Delisle, J. (2011). *The gifted teen survival guide* (4th ed.). Minneapolis, MN: Free Spirit.

Gallagher, J. J. (1975). *Teaching the gifted child* (2nd ed.). Boston, MA: Allyn & Bacon.

Gallagher, J. J. (2013). Educational disarmament, and how to stop it. *Roeper Review, 35,* 197–204.

Gardner, H. (1983). *Frames of mind*. New York, NY: Basic Books.

Gardner, J. W. (1961). *Excellence: Can we be equal and excellent, too?* New York, NY: W. W. Norton.

Gelb, M. J. (2004). *How to think like Leonardo da Vinci*. New York, NY: Bantam-Dell.

Gewertz, C., & Ujifusa, A. (2014). State plans for testing fragmented. *Education Week, 33,* 1, 16.

Gilman, B. J., Lovecky, D. V., Kearney, K., Peters, D. B., Wasserman, J. D., Silverman, L. K., . . . Rimm, S. B. (2013, July–September). Critical issues in the identification of gifted students with co-existing disabilities: The twice-exceptional. *SAGE Open,* 1–16.

Ginnott, H. G. (1972). *Teacher and child: A book for parents and teachers*. New York, NY: Macmillan.

Gladwell, M. (2008). *Outliers: The story of success*. New York, NY: Little Brown.

Gladwell, M. (2013). *David and Goliath: Underdogs, misfits, and the art of battling giants.* New York, NY: Little Brown.

Goodlad, J. (2003). A nation in wait. *Education Week.* Retrieved from http://www.edweek.org/ew/articles/2003/04/23/32goodlad. h22.html?qs=john+goodlad

Grennon Brooks, J., & Dietz, M. E. (2012). The dangers and opportunities of the Common Core. *Educational Leadership, 70*(4), 64–67.

Hargrove, K. (2013). Exam schools: Are they the solution for gifted students? *Gifted Child Today, 36*(1), 68–70.

Harrison, C. (2003). Giftedness in early childhood: The search for complexity and connection. *Roeper Review, 26*(2), 78–84.

Hartocollis, A. (2012). When pineapple races hare, students lose, critics of standardized tests say. *The New York Times.* Retrieved from http://www.nytimes.com/2012/04/21/nyregion/standardized-testing-is-blamed-for-question-about-a-sleeveless-pineapple.html

Henderson, M. (2010). *Some are born great.* Retrieved from http://spectator.co.uk/books/6025413/some-are-born-great/

Hernandez, B. (2012). *Is homeschool for you: 10 things to consider.* Retrieved from http://homeschooling.about.com/od/getting started/a/homeschool4you.htm

Hill, J. G., & Gruber, K. J. (2011). *Education and certification qualifications of departmentalized public high school-level teachers of core subjects: Statistical analysis report.* Washington, DC: U.S. Department of Education.

Hollingworth, L. S. (1942). *Children above 180 IQ-Stanford-Binet.* Yonkers-on-Hudson, NY: World Book Company.

Illinois Review. (2011). *NEA stands firm on homeschool regs.* Retrieved from http://www.illinoisreview.typepad.com/illinois review/2011/08/nea-stands-firm-on-homeschool-regs.html

Institute for Educational Advancement. (n.d.). *Caroline D. Bradley scholarship.* Retrieved from http://www.educationaladvancement. org/programs/caroline-d-bradley- scholarship

International Baccalaureate. (n.d.). *Mission and strategy.* Retrieved from https://www.ibo.org/mission

Isaacs, A. (1971). Preface. In J. C. Gowan & E. P. Torrance (Eds.), *Educating the ablest: A book of readings on the education of gifted children* (pp. iii–iv). Itasca, IL: F.E. Peacock.

Jacobs, H. H. (2010). *Curriculum 21: Essential education for a changing world.* Alexandria, VA: Association for Supervision and Curriculum Development.

Jacobs, J. (2010). *Can differentiation work?* Retrieved from http://www.joannejacobs.com/2010/11/can-differentiation-work

Jaschik, S. (2010). *AP: Good but oversold?* Retrieved from http://www.insidehighered.com/news/2010/03/30/ap

Johnsen, S. K. (2011). *NAGC Pre-K–Grade 12 gifted education programming standards: A guide to planning and implementing high-quality services.* Waco, TX: Prufrock Press.

Kaufman, S. B. (2012). Who is currently identified as gifted in the United States? *Psychology Today.* Retrieved from http://www.psychologytoday.com/blog/beautiful-minds/201201/who-is-currently-identified-gifted-in-the-united-states

Kearney, K. (1992). Homeschooling highly gifted children. *Understanding Our Gifted, 5*(1), 16.

Kearney, K. (1993). Discrimination against excellence. *Understanding Our Gifted, 6*(2), 16.

Kearney, K. (1996). Highly gifted children in full inclusion classrooms. *Highly Gifted Children, 12*(4), 1–4.

Kell, H. J., Lubinski, D., & Benbow, C. P. (2013). Who rises to the top? Early indicators. *Psychological Science, 24,* 648–659.

Koebler, J. (2011). Experts: STEM education is all about jobs. *U.S. News & World Report.* Retrieved from http://usnews.com/news/blogs/stem-education/2011/09/27

Kohn, A. (1998). Only for *my* kid: How privileged parents undermine school reform. *Phi Delta Kappan, 79,* 569–577.

Kornhaber, M., Fierros, E., & Veenema, S. (2004). *Multiple intelligences: Best ideas from research and practice.* Boston, MA: Allyn & Bacon.

Kristof, G. (2012). Common Core math in North Carolina would keep elementary students from taking middle school courses. *Huffington Post Education.* Retrieved from http://www.huffingtonpost.com/2012/05/30/wake-education_n_1556315.html

Kulik, J. Q. (1992). *An analysis of the research on ability grouping* (ERIC Documentation Reproduction Service No. ED350777). Storrs: University of Connecticut, The National Research Center on the Gifted and Talented.

Lakhan, S. E., & Laird, C. (2009). Addressing the primary care physician shortage in an evolving medical workforce. *International Archives of Medicine, 2,* 14.

Leslie, M. (2000). *The vexing legacy of Lewis Terman.* Retrieved from http://alumni.stanford.edu/get/page/magazine/article/?article_id=40678

Loveless, T. (2013). *How well are American students learning?* Washington, DC: Brookings Institute.

Marland, S. P., Jr. (1972). *Education of the gifted and talented: Report to the Congress of the United States by the U.S. Commissioner of Education and background papers submitted to the U.S. Office of Education,* 2 vols. Washington, DC: U.S. Government Printing Office. (Government Documents, Y4.L 11/2: G36)

Mathews, J. (2010). The untruth about the International Baccalaureate. *Washington Post.* Retrieved from http://voices.washingtonpost.com/class-struggle/2010/07/post_5.html

McBee, M. T., McCoach, D. B., Peters, S. J., & Matthews, M. S. (2012). The case for a schism: A commentary on Subotnik, Olszewski-Kubilius, and Worrell. *Gifted Child Quarterly, 56,* 210–214.

McClain, M. C., & Pfeiffer, S. (2012). Identification of gifted students in the United States today: A look at state definitions and practices. *Journal of Applied School Psychology, 28,* 59–88.

Meckstroth, E. A., & Kearney, K. (2013). Indecent exposure: Does the media exploit highly gifted children? In C. Neville, M. M. Piechowski, & S. Tolan (Eds.), *Off the charts: Asynchrony and the gifted child* (pp. 282–291). Unionville, NY: Royal Fireworks Press.

Morelock, M. J. (1992). Giftedness: The view from within. *Understanding Our Gifted, 4*(2), 1, 11–15.

National Association for Gifted Children. (1991). *NAGC position statement: Ability grouping.* Retrieved from http://www.nagc.org/index/aspx?id=382

National Association for Gifted Children. (2008). *NAGC position statement: Use of the WISC-IV for gifted identification*. Washington, DC: Author.

National Association for Gifted Children. (2010). *What is giftedness?* Retrieved from http://www.nagc.org/WhatisGiftedness.aspx

National Association for Gifted Children. (2013). *State of the nation in gifted education: Work yet to be done*. Washington, DC: Author.

National Association for Gifted Children, & National Middle School Association. (2005). *Meeting the needs of high ability learners in the middle grades*. Retrieved from http://www.nagc.org/index. aspx?id=400

National Association for Gifted Children, & The Association for the Gifted, Council for Exceptional Children. (2006). *NAGC-CEC teacher knowledge and skill standards for gifted and talented education*. Retrieved from http://www.nagc.org/uploadedFiles/ Information_and_Resources/NCATE_standards/final%20 standards%20(2006).pdf

National Center for Response to Intervention. (n.d.). *What is RTI?* Retrieved from http://www.rti4success.org

National Commission on Excellence in Education. (1983). *A nation at risk*. Washington, DC: U.S. Government Printing Office.

National Governors Association Center for Best Practices, & Council of Chief State School Officers. (2010a). *English/Language arts standards*. Retrieved from http://www.corestandards.org/ ela-literacy

National Governors Association Center for Best Practices, & Council of Chief State School Officers. (2010b). *English/Language arts standards: Introduction: Key design consideration*. Retrieved from http://www.corestandards.org/ela-literacy/introduction/key-design-consideration

Neal, D., & Schanzenbach, D. W. (2007). Left behind by design: Proficiency counts and test-based accountability. *Social Science Research Network*. Retrieved from http://papers.ssrn.com/sol3/ papers.cfm?abstract_id=1005606

Oakes, J. (2005). *Keeping track: How schools structure inequality* (2nd ed.). New Haven, CT: Yale University Press.

Olszewski-Kubilius, P. (2011). Taking a bold step. *Compass Points, 4*(11), 1–2.

Organization for Economic Cooperation and Development. (2012). *Education at a glance 2012: OECD indicators.* Retrieved from http://www.oecd.org/edu/EAG%202012_e-book_EN_200912. pdf

Parsad, B., & Spiegelman-Westat, M. (2012). *Arts education in public elementary and secondary schools, 1999-2000 and 2009-2010.* Washington, DC: U.S. Department of Education.

Passow, A. H. (1979). *The gifted and talented: Their education and development.* Chicago, IL: National Society for the Study of Education.

Pegnato, C. W., & Birch, J. W. (1959). Locating gifted children in junior high schools: A comparison of methods. *Exceptional Children, 25,* 300–304.

Porter, A. C. (2011). In Common Core, little to cheer about. *Education Week, 30*(37), 24–25.

Prensky, M. (2014). The goal of education is becoming. *Education Week, 33,* 36, 40.

Raiford, S. E., Weiss, L. G., Rolfhus, E., & Coalson, D. (2008). *WISC-IV: General ability index* (Technical Report #4). Retrieved from http:// www.pearsonassessments.com/NR/rdonlyres/1439CDFE-6980-435F-93DA-05888C7CC082/0/80720_WISCIV_Hr_ r4.pdf

Rapaport, A. (2013). *A standardized testing revolt.* Retrieved from http://www.prospect.org/article/standardized-testing-revolt

Ravitch, D. (2010). *Death and life of the great American school system: How testing and choice are undermining education.* New York, NY: Basic Books.

Ravitch, D. (2012). *How testing reduces instructional time.* Retrieved from http://dianeravitch.net/2012/09/28/how-testing-reduces-instructional-time

Ravitch, D. (2013). *Reign of error: The hoax of the privatization movement and the danger to America's public schools.* New York, NY: Knopf.

Renzulli, J. S. (1977). *The Enrichment Triad Model: A guide for developing defensible programs for the gifted and talented.* Waco, TX: Prufrock Press.

Renzulli, J. S. (1978). What makes giftedness?: Reexamining a definition. *Phi Delta Kappan, 60,* 180–184, 261.

Ripley, A. (2012, Oct.). Why kids should grade teachers. *The Atlantic,* 88–93.

Robinson, N. (1993). *Parenting the very young, gifted child* (RBDM 9308). Storrs: University of Connecticut, The National Research Center on the Gifted and Talented.

Roeper, A. (1982). How the gifted cope with their emotions. *Roeper Review, 5*(2), 21.

Roeper. A. (1991). Gifted adults: Their characteristics and emotions. *Advanced Development, 3,* 85–98.

Roeper, A. (2004). The Annemarie Roeper Method of Qualitative Assessment. *Gifted Education Communicator, 35*(3), 31–33.

Roeper, A. (2007). *The "I" of the beholder: A guided journey to the essence of a child.* Scottsdale, AZ: Great Potential Press.

Roeper, A. (n.d.). *Qualitative assessment: An alternative to the IQ test.* Retrieved from http://www.gifteddevelopment.com/PDF files/ AMR%20.Symposium%20Paper.pdf

Sadler, P. M., Sonnert, G., Tai, R. H., & Klopfenstein, K. (2010). *AP: A critical examination of the Advanced Placement program.* Cambridge, MA: Harvard University Press.

Sapon-Shevin, M. (1994). Why gifted students belong in inclusive schools. *Educational Leadership, 52*(4), 64–70.

Saul, S. (2011). Profits and questions at online charter schools. *The New York Times.* Retrieved from http://nytimes.com/2011/12/13/ education

Schaeffer, B. (2012). *Resistance to high stakes testing spreads.* Retrieved from http://www.districtadministration.com/article/ resistance-high-stakes-testing-spreads

Scharfenberg, D. (2007). Scarsdale seeks alternative to Advanced Placement. *The New York Times.* Retrieved from http://www. nytimes.com/2007/02/18/nyregion/nyregionspecial2/18we topic.html_r=0

Schiller, J., & Arena, C. (2012). How corporations are helping to solve the education crisis. *Co.EXIST.* Retrieved from http://www.fastcoexist.com/1679529/how-corporations-are-helping-to-solve-the-education-crisis

Schmoker, M. (2010). When pedagogic fads trump priorities. *Education Week, 30*(5), 2S.

Schroeder-Davis, S. (2012). Why don't our schools graduate more intellectuals? *Gifted Education Press Quarterly, 26*(4), 2–7.

Schroeder-Davis, S. (2013). Intellectualism. *Gifted Education Press Quarterly, 27*(2), 8–13.

Schultz. B. (2011, Summer). A conversation somewhere in time. *Teaching for High Potential, 16,* 19.

Schultz, B. (2012, Summer). STEM, STEMM, or STEAM? *Teaching for High Potential,* 9.

Schultz, R. A., & Delisle, J. R. (2012). *If I'm so smart, why aren't the answers easy?* Waco, TX: Prufrock Press.

Schwinger, E., & Delisle, J. (2012). Gaining wisdom by giving back: Helping gifted young people help others. *Gifted Education Communicator, 43*(3), 15–18.

Seward, K. (2004). Back to the future: The Personalized Education Process (PEP). *Understanding Our Gifted, 16*(3), 12–13.

Shanahan, T. (2012/2013). The Common Core ate my baby and other urban legends. *Educational Leadership, 70*(4), 10–16.

Shanker, A. (1994). Full inclusion is neither free nor appropriate. *Educational Leadership, 52*(4), 18–21.

Shenk, D. (2010). *The genius in all of us: Why everything you've been told about genetics, talent, and IQ is wrong.* New York, NY: Doubleday.

Siegle, D. (2007). *Gifted children's bill of rights.* Washington, DC: National Association for Gifted Children.

Silverman, L. (n.d.). *Asynchrony: A new definition of giftedness.* Retrieved from http://www.tip.duke.edu/node/839

Silverman, L. K., Gilman, B., & Falk, R. F. (n.d.). *Who are the gifted using the new WISC-IV?* Retrieved from http://www.gifteddevelopment.com/PDF_files/NewWisc.pdf

Speirs Neumeister, K. (2012). *In response to* A Defining Moment. Retrieved from http://www.hoagiesgifted.org/response_defining_moment.htm

Stainback, W., & Stainback, S. (1990). *Support networks for inclusive schooling: Interdependent integrated education.* Baltimore, MD: Brookes.

Stephens, K., & Riggsbee, J. (2007). *The children neglected by No Child Left Behind.* Retrieved from http://www.today.duke.edu/2007/02/gifted_oped.html

Strauss, V. (2010). The problems with the Common Core Standards. *Washington Post.* Retrieved from http://voices.washingtonpost.com/answer-sheet/national-standards/the-problems-with-the-common-core.html

Strauss, V. (2011). A Texas superintendent's testing dilemma. *Washington Post.* Retrieved from http://www.washingtonpost.com/blogs/answer-sheet/post/a-texas/superintendents-testing-dilemma/2011/04/16

Strauss, V. (2012). Texas GOP rejects 'critical thinking' skills. Really. *Washington Post.* Retrieved from http://www.washingtonpost.com/blogs/answer-sheet/post/texas-gop-rejects-critical-thinking-skills-really/2012/07/08/gJQAHNpFXW_blog.html

Strauss, V. (2013a). *Atlanta test cheating: Tip of the iceberg?* Retrieved from http://www.commondreams.org/view/2013/04/01-5

Strauss, V. (2013b). Common Core supporters back moratorium on new tests' high stakes. *Washington Post.* Retrieved from http://www.washingtonpost.com/blogs/answer-sheet/wp/2013/06/06/common-core-supporters-back-moratorium-on-new-tests-high-stakes/

Subotnik, R. F., Olzsewski-Kubilius, P., & Worrell, F. C. (2011). Rethinking giftedness and gifted education: A proposed direction forward based on psychological science. *Gifted Child Quarterly, 56,* 176–188.

Syed, M. (2010). *Bounce: Mozart, Federer, Picasso, Beckham, and the science of success.* New York, NY: HarperCollins.

TED. (n.d.). *History.* Retrieved from http://www.ted.com/pages/16

Terman, L. M. (1954). The discovery and encouragement of exceptional talent. *American Psychologist, 9,* 221–230.

Thornburg, J. C. (2004, September 27). Saving the smart kids. *TIME,* 56–59.

U.S. Department of Education. (2008). *A nation accountable: 25 years after A Nation At Risk.* Retrieved from http://www.edgov/rschstat/research/pubs/accountable

Vander-Hart, S. (2012). *Arne Duncan, the Common Core bully.* Retrieved from http://caffeinatedthoughts.com/2012/02/arne-duncan-the-common-core-bully/

VanTassel-Baska, J. (2012). A case for Common Core State Standards. *Gifted Child Today, 35,* 222–223.

Ward, V. S. (1961). *Educating the gifted: An axiomatic approach.* Columbus, OH: Charles E. Merrill.

Wells, A. S., & Serna, I. (1996). The politics of culture: Understanding local political resistance to detracking in racially mixed schools. *Harvard Educational Review, 66,* 93–118.

Welsh, P. (2009). *The Advanced Placement juggernaut.* Retrieved from http://roomfordebate.blogs.nytimes.com/2009/12/20/the-advanced-placement-juggernaut

Wesling, S. (2010). *Book review: The Genius in All of Us.* Retrieved from http://www.examiner.com/article/book-review-the-genius-in-all-of-us

Wheelock, A. (1995). Winning over gifted parents. *School Administrator, 52*(4), 16–20.

White, M. (2012). *New options emerge to enrich gifted students' education.* Retrieved from http://deseretnews.com/article/765588153/New-options-emerge-to-enrich-gifted-students-education.html?pg=all

Whitmore, J. R. (1980). *Giftedness, conflict and underachievement.* Boston, MA: Allyn & Bacon.

Wilemon, T. (2013). *Born in prison, Arkansas student now excels at Vanderbilt.* Retrieved from http://www.usatoday.com/story/news/nation/2013/12/27/science-medical-scholarship-disadvantaged-student/4218019

Willingham, D. (2004, Summer). Reframing the mind. *Education Next*, 19–24.

Zhu, J., Cayton, T., Weiss, L., & Gabel, A. (2008). *WISC-IV extended norms* (Technical Report #7). Retrieved from http://images. pearsonclinical.com/images/assets/WISC-IV/WISCIV_ TechReport_7.pdf

ABOUT THE AUTHOR

Dr. James Delisle has been an advocate of gifted children for more than 35 years and is a frequent thorn in the side to those who deny gifted kids a place at the education table. As a teacher, author, professor, and dad, Jim has learned that gifted children have as much a right to an appropriate education as any other child. He is sick and tired of America's dumbed down education system and hopes that this book—his 19th—helps to reverse that trend.

INDEX